Allyn and Bacon

Research Navigator Guide

Special Education

Judith Osgood Smith
Purdue University–Calumet

Linda R. Barr
University of the Virgin Islands

PEARSON

Boston | New York | San Francisco
Mexico City | Montreal | Toronto | London | Madrid | Munich | Paris
Hong Kong | Singapore | Tokyo | Cape Town | Sydney

Contents

Introduction

Your professor assigns a research paper or group report that's due in two weeks—and you need to make sure you have up-to-date, credible information. Where do you begin? Today, the easiest answer is the Internet—because it can be so convenient and there is so much information out there. But therein lies part of the problem. How do you know if the information is reliable and from a trustworthy source?

Research Navigator Guide: Special Education is designed to help you select and evaluate research from the Web to help you find the best and most credible information you can. Throughout this guide, you'll find:

- **A Quick Guide to Research Navigator.** All you need to know to get started with Research Navigator™, a research database that gives you immediate access to hundreds of scholarly journals and other popular publications, such as *Scientific American, U.S. News & World Report,* and many others.
- **A practical and to-the-point discussion of search engines.** Find out which search engines are likely to get you the information you want and how to phrase your searches for the most effective results.
- **Detailed information on evaluating online sources.** Locate credible information on the Web and get tips for thinking critically about Web sites.
- **Citation guidelines for Web resources.** Learn the proper citation guidelines for Web sites, email messages, listservs, and more.
- **Web activities for Special Education.** Explore the various ways you can use the Web in your courses through these online exercises.
- **Web links for Special Education.** Begin your Web research with the discipline-specific sources listed in this section. Also included is information about Web resources offered by Allyn & Bacon—these sites are designed to give you an extra boost in your special education courses.

So before running straight to your browser, take the time to read through this copy of *Research Navigator Guide: Special Education* and use it as a reference for all of your Web research needs.

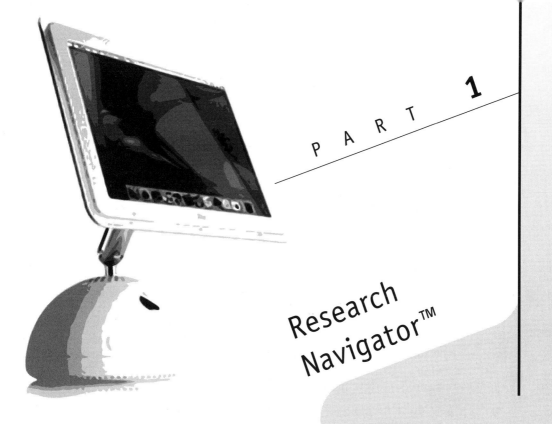

Research
Navigator™

What Is Research Navigator™?

Research Navigator™ is the easiest way for you to start a research assignment or paper.

Research Navigator™ includes three databases of dependable source material to get your research process started:

1. EBSCO's ContentSelect™ Academic Journal and Abstract Database, organized by subject, contains 50–100 of the leading academic journals per discipline. Instructors and students can search the online journals by keyword, topic, or multiple topics. Articles include abstract and citation information and can be cut, pasted, emailed, or saved for later use.

2. The *New York Times* Search by Subject Archive is organized by academic subject and searchable by keyword, or multiple keywords. Instructors and students can view full-text articles from the world's leading journalists from *The New York Times*. The *New York Times* Search by Subject Archive is available exclusively to instructors and students through Research Navigator™.

3. Link Library, organized by subject, offers editorially selected "Best of the Web" sites. Link libraries are continually scanned and kept up to date, providing the most relevant and accurate links for research assignments.

In addition, Research Navigator™ includes extensive online content detailing the steps in the research process including:

- Starting the Research Process
- Finding and Evaluating Sources
- Citing Sources
- Internet Research
- Using your Library
- Starting to Write

To begin using Research Navigator™, you must first register using the personal access code that appears in the front cover of this book. Follow the registration instructions on the inside front cover.

Getting Started

From the Research Navigator™ homepage, you have easy access to all of the site's main features, including a quick route to the three exclusive databases of source content that will be discussed in greater detail on the following pages. If you are new to the research process, you may want to start by clicking the *Research Process* tab, located in the upper right hand section of the page. Here you will find extensive help on all aspects of the research process, including:

- Introduction to the Research Paper
- Gathering Data

- Searching the Internet
- Evaluating Sources
- Organizing Ideas
- Writing Notes
- Drafting the Paper
- Academic Citation Styles (MLA, APA, CME, and more)
- Blending Reference Material into Your Writing
- Practicing Academic Integrity
- Revising
- Proofreading
- Editing the Final Draft

For those of you who are already familiar with the research process, you already know that the first step in completing a research assignment or research paper is to select a topic. (In some cases, your instructor may assign you a topic.) According to James D. Lester in *Writing Research Papers,* choosing a topic for the research paper can be easy (any topic will serve) yet very complicated (an informed choice is critical). He suggests selecting a person, a person's work, or a specific issue to study—President George W. Bush, John Steinbeck's *Of Mice and Men,* or learned dexterity with Nintendo games. Try to select a topic that will meet three demands.

1. It must examine a significant issue.
2. It must address a knowledgeable reader and carry that reader to another level of knowledge.
3. It must have a serious purpose, one that demands analysis of the issues, argues from a position, and explains complex details.

You can find more tips from Lester in the *Research Process* section of Research Navigator™.

EBSCO's ContentSelect Academic Journal and Abstract Database

EBSCO's ContentSelect Academic Journal and Abstract Database contains scholarly, peer-reviewed journals (such as the *Journal of Clinical Psychology*). A scholarly journal is an edited collection of articles written by various authors and is published several times per year. All the issues published in one calendar year comprise a volume of that journal. For example, the *American Sociological Review* published volume 65 in the year 2000. This journal is published six times a year, so issues 1–6 in volume 65 are the individual issues for that year. Each issue contains between 4 and 8 articles. Additionally, issues may contain letters from the editor, book reviews, and comments from authors. Each issue does not necessarily revolve around a common theme; most issues contain articles on many different topics.

Although similar to magazines in that they are published several times per year and contain articles on different topics, scholarly journals are NOT magazines. What sets them apart from popular magazines is that the content of each issue is peer-reviewed. The editor relies on these peer reviewers both to evaluate the articles and to decide if they should be accepted for publication. Academic journal articles adhere to strict scientific guidelines for methodology and theoretical grounding. The information in these articles is more scientific than information in a popular magazine, newspaper article, or on a Web page.

Using ContentSelect.   Here are some instructions and search tips to help you find articles for your research paper.

Step 1: **Select an academic subject and topic area.** When you first enter the database, you will see a list of disciplines. To search within a single academic subject, click the name of that subject. To search in more than one subject, hold down the alt or command key. In the space below where all the subjects are listed, enter a topic area. For example if you choose Psychology as a subject you might enter "Freud" as a topic area.

Step 2: **Basic Search.** Click the **GO** button to start your search. You will be brought to the *Basic Search* tab. Basic Search lets you search for articles using a variety of methods. You can select from: Standard Search, All Words, Any Words, or Exact Phrase. For more information on these options, click the **Search Tips** link at any time! After you have selected your method click **Search.**

Some ways to improve your search:

Tip 1: **AND, OR, and NOT**. In Standard Search, you can use AND, OR and NOT to create a broad or narrow search:

- **AND** searches for articles containing all of the words. For example, typing **education AND technology** will search for articles that contain **both** education AND technology.
- **OR** searches for articles that contains at least one of the terms. For example, searching for **education OR technology** will find articles that contain either education OR technology.
- **NOT** excludes words so that the articles will not include the word that follows "NOT." For example, searching for **education NOT technology** will find articles that contain the term education but NOT the term technology.

Tip 2: **Using All Words.** When you select the "All Words" option, you do not need to use the word AND—you will automatically search for articles that only contain all of the words. The order of the search words entered in does not matter. For example, typing **education technology** will search for articles that contain **both** education AND technology.

Tip 3: **Using Any Words.** After selecting the "Any Words" option, type words, a phrase, or a sentence in the window. ContentSelect will search for articles that contain any of the terms you typed (but will not search for words such as **in** and **the**). For example, type **rising medical costs in the United States** to find articles that contain *rising, medical, costs, United,* or *States.* To limit your search to find articles that contain exact terms, use *quotation marks*—for example, typing "United States" will only search for articles containing "United States."

Tip 4: **Using Exact Phrase.** Select this option to find articles containing an exact phrase. ContentSelect will search for articles that include all the words you entered, exactly as you entered them. For example, type **rising medical costs in the United States** to find articles that contain the exact phrase "rising medical costs in the United States."

Search by Article Number.

Each and every article in EBSCO's ContentSelect Academic Journal and Abstract Database is assigned its own unique article number. In some instances, you may know the exact article number for the journal article you want to retrieve. Perhaps you noted it during a prior research session on Research Navigator™. Such article numbers might also be found on the companion web site for your text, or in the text itself.

To retrieve a specific article, simply type that article number in the "Search by Article Number" field and click the **GO** button.

Advanced Search.

These tips will help you with an Advanced Search.

Step 1: To switch to an **Advanced Search**, from the Basic Search click the *AdvancedSearch* tab on the navigation bar, just under the EBSCO Host logo. The *AdvancedSearch* tab helps you focus your search using key-word searching, search history and limiters.

Step 2: Type the words you want to search for in the **Find** field.

Step 3: Click on **Field Codes** to see a list of available field codes for lim-iting your search. For example: AU-Author, will limit your search to an author. Enter one of these two-letter field codes before your search term. For example, if you enter AU-Smith, this will limit your results to SMITH in the Author field. For more information on field codes, click **Search Tips**. After you have added the appropriate Field Code to your topic, click **Search.**

Some ways to improve your search:

Tip 1: You can enter additional search terms in the **Find** field, and re-member to use *and, or,* and *not* to connect multiple search terms (see Tip 1 under Basic Search for information on *and, or,* and *not*).

Tip 2: With Advanced Searches you can also use **Limiters** and **Expanders** to refine your search. For more information on Limiters and Expanders, click **Search Tips**.

The *New York Times* Search by Subject Archive

Newspapers, also known as periodicals because they are issued in periodic installments (e.g. daily, weekly, or monthly), provide contemporary informa-tion. Information in periodicals—journals, magazines, and newspapers—may be useful, or even critical, when you are ready to focus in on specific aspects of your topic, or to find more up-to-date information.

There are some significant differences between newspaper articles and journal articles, and you should consider the level of scholarship that is most appropriate for your research. Popular or controversial topics may not be well covered in journals, even though coverage in newspapers and "general interest" magazines like *Newsweek* and *Science* for that same topic may be extensive.

Research Navigator™ gives you access to a one-year, "search by subject" archive of articles from *The New York Times*. To learn more about *The New York Times,* visit **http://www.nytimes.com**.

Using the search-by-subject archive is easy. Simply type a word, or multiple words separated by commas, into the search box and click "go." You will see a list of articles that have appeared in the *New York Times* over the last year, sorted by most recent article first. You can further refine your search as needed. Articles can be printed or saved for later use in your re-search assignment. Be sure to review the citation rules for how to cite a newspaper article in endnotes or a bibliography.

Research Navigator Guide: Special Education

"Best of the Web" Link Library

The third database included on Research Navigator™, Link Library, is a collection of Web links, organized by academic subject and key terms. To use this database, simply select an academic subject from the dropdown list, and then find the key term for the topic you are searching. Click on the key term and see a list of five to seven editorially reviewed Web sites that offer educationally relevant and reliable content. For example, if your research topic is "Allergies," you may want to select the academic subject Biology and then click on "Allergies" for links to web sites that explore this topic. Simply click on the alphabet bar to view other key terms in Biology, and their corresponding links. The web links in Link Library are monitored and updated each week, reducing your incidence of finding "dead" links.

Using Your Library

After you have selected your topic and gathered source material from the three databases of content on Research Navigator™, you may need to complete your research by going to your school library. Research Navigator™ does not try to replace the library, but rather helps you understand how to use library resources effectively and efficiently.

You may put off going to the library to complete research assignments or research papers because the library can seem overwhelming. Research Navigator™ provides a bridge to the library by taking you through a simple step-by-step overview of how to make the most of your library time. Written by a library scientist, the *Using Your Library* tab explains:

- Major types of libraries
- What the library has to offer
- How to choose the right library tools for a project
- The research process
- How to make the most of research time in the library

In addition, when you are ready to use the library to complete a research assignment or research paper, Research Navigator™ includes 31 discipline-specific "library guides" for you to use as a roadmap. Each guide includes an overview of the discipline's major subject databases, online journals, and key associations and newsgroups.

For more information and detailed walk-throughs, please visit
www.ablongman.com/aboutRN

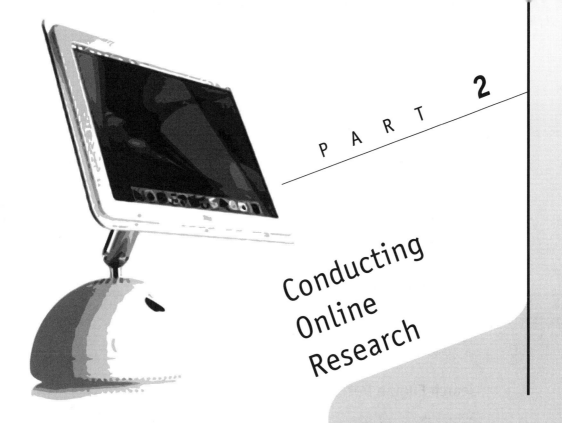

PART 2

Conducting
Online
Research

Finding Sources:
Search Engines and Subject Directories

Your professor has just given you an assignment to give a five minute speech on the topic "gun control." After a (hopefully brief) panic attack, you begin to think of what type of information you need before you can write the speech. To provide an interesting introduction, you decide to involve your class by taking a straw poll of their views for and against gun control, and to follow this up by giving some statistics on how many Americans favor (and oppose) gun control legislation and then by outlining the arguments on both sides of the issue. If you already know the correct URL for an authoritative Web site like Gallup Opinion Polls (www.gallup.com) or other sites you are in great shape! However, what do you do when you don't have a clue as to which Web site would have information on your topic? In these cases, many, many people routinely (and mistakenly) go to Yahoo! and type in a single term (e.g., guns). This approach is sure to bring first a smile to your face when the results offer you 200,874 hits on your topic, but just as quickly make you grind your teeth in frustration when you start scrolling down the hit list and find sites that range from gun dealerships, to reviews of the video "Young Guns," to aging fan sites for "Guns and Roses."

Finding information on a specific topic on the Web is a challenge. The more intricate your research need, the more difficult it is to find the one or two Web sites among the billions that feature the information you want. This section is designed to help you to avoid frustration and to focus in on the right site for your research by using search engines, subject directories, and meta-sites.

Search Engines

Search engines (sometimes called search services) are becoming more numerous on the Web. Originally, they were designed to help users search the Web by topic. More recently, search engines have added features which enhance their usefulness, such as searching a particular part of the Web (e.g., only sites of educational institutions—dot.edu), retrieving just one site which the search engine touts as most relevant (like Ask Jeeves {www.aj.com}), or retrieving up to 10 sites which the search engine rank as most relevant (like Google {www.google.com}).

Search Engine Defined

According to Cohen (1999):

> "A search engine service provides a searchable database of Internet files collected by a computer program called a wanderer, crawler, robot, worm, or spider. Indexing is created from the collected files, and the results are presented in a schematic order. There are no selection criteria for the collection of files.
>
> A search service therefore consists of three components: (1) a spider, a program that traverses the Web from link to link, identifying and reading pages; (2) an index, a database containing a copy of each Web page gathered by the spider; and (3) a search engine mechanism, software that enables users to query the index and then returns results in a schematic order (p. 31)."

One problem students often have in their use of search engines is that they are deceptively easy to use. Like our example "guns," no matter what is typed into the handy box at the top, links to numerous Web sites appear instantaneously, lulling students into a false sense of security. Since so much was retrieved, surely SOME of it must be useful. WRONG! Many Web sites retrieved will be very light on substantive content, which is not what you need for most academic endeavors. Finding just the right Web site has been likened to finding diamonds in the desert.

As you can see by the definition above, one reason for this is that most search engines use indexes developed by machines. Therefore they are indexing terms not concepts. The search engine cannot tell the difference between the keyword "crack" to mean a split in the sidewalk and "crack" referring to crack cocaine. To use search engines properly takes some skill, and this chapter will provide tips to help you use search engines more effectively. First, however, let's look at the different types of search engines with examples:

TYPES OF SEARCH ENGINES		
TYPE	DESCRIPTION	EXAMPLES
1st Generation	• Non-evaluative, do not evaluate results in terms of content or authority. • Return results ranked by relevancy alone (number of times the term(s) entered appear, usually on the first paragraph or page of the site)	AltaVista (www.altavista.com/) Excite (www.excite.com) HotBot (www.HotBot.com) Infoseek (guide.infoseek.com) Ixquick Metasearch (ixquick.com) Lycos (www.lycos.com)
2nd Generation	• More creative in displaying results. • Results are ordered by characteristics such as: concept, document type, Web site, popularity, etc. rather than relevancy.	Ask Jeeves (www.aj.com/) Direct Hit (www.directhit.com/) Google! (www.google.com/) HotLinks (www.hotlinks.com/) Simplifind (www.simpli.com/) SurfWax (www.surfwax.com/) Also see Meta-Search engines below. EVALUATIVE SEARCH ENGINES About.Com (www.about.com) WebCrawler (www.webcrawler.com)
Commercial Portals	• Provide additional features such as: customized news, stock quotations, weather reports, shopping, etc. • They want to be used as a "one stop" Web guide. • They profit from prominent advertisements and fees charged to featured sites.	GONetwork (www.go.com/) Google Web Directory (directory.google.com/) LookSmart (www.looksmart.com/) My Starting Point (www.stpt.com/) Open Directory Project (dmoz.org/) NetNow (www.inetnow.com) Yahoo! (www.yahoo.com/)
Meta-Search Engines	Run searches on multiple search engines.	There are different types of meta-search engines. See the next 2 boxes.

(continued)

TYPES OF SEARCH ENGINES, *continued*		
TYPE	DESCRIPTION	EXAMPLES
Meta-Search Engines *Integrated Result*	• Display results for search engines in one list. • Duplicates are removed. • Only portions of results from each engine are returned.	Beaucoup.com (www.beaucoup.com/) Highway 61 (www.highway61.com) Cyber411(www.cyber411. com/) Mamma (www.mamma.com/) MetaCrawler (www. metacrawler.com/) Visisimo (www.vivisimo.com) Northern Light (www.nlsearch.com/) SurfWax (www.surfwax.com)
Meta-Search Engines *Non-Integrated Results*	• Comprehensive search. • Displays results from each search engine in separate results sets. • Duplicates remain. • You must sift through all the sites.	Dogpile (www.dogpile.com) Global Federated Search (jin.dis.vt.edu/fedsearch/) GoHip (www.gohip.com) Searchalot (www.searchalot.com) 1Blink (www.1blink.com) ProFusion (www. profusion.com/)

QUICK TIPS FOR MORE EFFECTIVE USE OF SEARCH ENGINES

1. Use a search engine:
   - When you have a narrow idea to search.
   - When you want to search the full text of countless Web pages
   - When you want to retrieve a large number of sites
   - When the features of the search engine (like searching particular parts of the Web) help with your search

2. Always use Boolean Operators to combine terms. Searching on a single term is a sure way to retrieve a very large number of Web pages, few, if any, of which are on target.
   - Always check search engine's HELP feature to see what symbols are used for the operators as these vary (e.g., some engines use the & or + symbol for AND).
   - Boolean Operators include:
     AND to narrow search and to make sure that **both** terms are included
       e.g:, children AND violence
     OR to broaden search and to make sure that **either** term is included
       e.g., child OR children OR juveniles
     NOT to **exclude** one term
       e.g., eclipse NOT lunar

3. Use appropriate symbols to indicate important terms and to indicate phrases (Best Bet for Constructing a Search According to Cohen (1999): Use a plus sign (+) in front of terms you want to retrieve: +solar +eclipse. Place a phrase in double quotation marks: "solar eclipse" Put together: "+solar eclipse" "+South America").

4. Use word stemming (a.k.a. truncation) to find all variations of a word (check search engine HELP for symbols).
   - If you want to retrieve child, child's, or children use child* (some engines use other symbols such as !, #, or $)
   - Some engines automatically search singular and plural terms, check HELP to see if yours does.

5. Since search engines only search a portion of the Web, use several search engines or a meta-search engine to extend your reach.

6. Remember search engines are generally mindless drones that do not evaluate. Do not rely on them to find the best Web sites on your topic, use *subject directories* or meta-sites to enhance value (see below).

Finding Those Diamonds in the Desert: Using Subject Directories and Meta-sites

Although some search engines, like WebCrawler (www.webcrawler.com) do evaluate the Web sites they index, most search engines do not make any judgment on the worth of the content. They just return a long—sometimes very long—list of sites that contained your keyword. However, *subject directories* exist that are developed by human indexers, usually librarians or subject experts, and are defined by Cohen (1999) as follows:

> "A subject directory is a service that offers a collection of links to Internet resources submitted by site creators or evaluators and organized into subject categories. Directory services use selection criteria for choosing links to include, though the selectivity varies among services (p. 27)."

World Wide Web Subject directories are useful when you want to see sites on your topic that have been reviewed, evaluated, and selected for their authority, accuracy, and value. They can be real time savers for students, since subject directories weed out the commercial, lightweight, or biased Web sites.

Metasites are similar to subject directories, but are more specific in nature, usually dealing with one scholarly field or discipline. Some examples of subject directories and meta-sites are found in the table on the next page.

Choose subject directories to ensure that you are searching the highest quality Web pages. As an added bonus, subject directories periodically check Web links to make sure that there are fewer dead ends and out-dated links.

SMART SEARCHING—SUBJECT DIRECTORIES AND META-SITES

TYPES—SUBJECT DIRECTORIES	EXAMPLES
General, covers many topics	Access to Internet and Subject Resources (www2.lib.udel.edu/subj/) Best Information on the Net (BIOTN) (http://library.sau.edu/bestinfo/) Federal Web Locator (www.infoctr.edu/fwl/) Galaxy (galaxy.einet.net) INFOMINE: Scholarly Internet Resource Collections (infomine.ucr.edu/) InfoSurf: Resources by Subject (www.library.ucsb.edu/subj/) Librarian's Index to the Internet (www.lii.org/) Martindale's "The Reference Desk" (www-sci.lib.uci.edu/HSG/ref.html) PINAKES: A Subject Launchpad (www.hw.ac.uk/libWWW/irn/pinakes/pinakes.html) Refdesk.com (www.refdesk.com) Search Engines and Subject Directories (College of New Jersey) (www.tcnj.edu/~library/research/internet_search.html) Scout Report Archives (www.scout.cs.wisc.edu/archives) Selected Reference Sites (www.mnsfld.edu/depts/lib/mu~ref.html) WWW Virtual Library (http://vlib.org)
Subject Oriented	
• Communication Studies	The Media and Communication Studies Site (www.aber.ac.uk/media) University of Iowa Department of Communication Studies (www.uiowa.edu/~commstud/resources)
• Cultural Studies	Sara Zupko's Cultural Studies Center (www.popcultures.com)
• Education	Educational Virtual Library (www.csu.edu.au/education/library.html) ERIC [Education ResourcesInformation Center] (ericir.sunsite.syr.edu/) Kathy Schrock's Guide for Educators (kathyschrock.net/abceval/index.htm)
• Journalism	Journalism Resources (bailiwick.lib.uiowa.edu/journalism/) Journalism and Media Criticism page (www.chss.montclair.edu/english/furr/media.html)
• Literature	Norton Web Source to American Literature (www.wwnorton.com/naal) Project Gutenberg [Over 3,000 full text titles] (www.gutenberg.net)

SMART SEARCHING, *continued*	
TYPES—SUBJECT DIRECTORIES	EXAMPLES
• Medicine & Health	PubMed [National Library of Medicine's index to Medical journals, 1966 to present] (www.ncbi.nlm.nih.gov/PubMed/) RxList: The Internet Drug Index (rxlist.com) Go Ask Alice (www.goaskalice.columbia.edu) [Health and sexuality]
• Technology	CNET.com (www.cnet.com)

Another closely related group of sites are the *Virtual Library sites,* also referred to as Digital Library sites. Hopefully, your campus library has an outstanding Web site for both on-campus and off-campus access to resources. If not, there are several virtual library sites that you can use, although you should realize that some of the resources would be subscription based, and not accessible unless you are a student of that particular university or college. These are useful because, like the subject directories and meta-sites, experts have organized Web sites by topic and selected only those of highest quality.

You now know how to search for information and use search engines more effectively. In the next section, you will learn more tips for evaluating the information that you found.

VIRTUAL LIBRARY SITES	
PUBLIC LIBRARIES	
• Internet Public Library • Library of Congress • New York Public Library	www.ipl.org lcweb.loc.gov/homepage/lchp.html www.nypl.org
University/College Libraries • Bucknell • Case Western • Dartmouth • Duke • Franklin & Marshall • Harvard • Penn State • Princeton • Stanford • ULCA	jade.bucknell.edu/ www.cwru.edu/uclibraries.html www.dartmouth.edu/~library www.lib.duke.edu/ www.library.fandm.edu www.harvard.edu/museums/ www.libraries.psu.edu infoshare1.princeton.edu www.slac.stanford.edu/FIND/spires.html www.library.ucla.edu

(continued)

Research Navigator Guide: Special Education

VIRTUAL LIBRARY SITES, *continued*

PUBLIC LIBRARIES

Other
- Perseus Project [subject specific—classics, supported by   www.perseus.tufts.edu
  grants from corporations and educational institutions]

BIBLIOGRAPHY FOR FURTHER READING

Books

Basch, Reva. (1996). Secrets of the Super Net Searchers.

Berkman, Robert I. (2000). *Find It Fast: How to Uncover Expert Information on Any Subject Online or in Print.* NY: HarperResource.

Glossbrenner, Alfred & Glossbrenner, Emily. (1999). *Search Engines for the World Wide Web,* 2nd Ed. Berkeley, CA: Peachpit Press.

Hock, Randolph, & Berinstein, Paula.. (1999). *The Extreme Searcher's Guide to Web Search Engines: A Handbook for the Serious Searcher.* Information Today, Inc.

Miller, Michael. *Complete Idiot's Guide to Yahoo!* (2000). Indianapolis, IN: Que.

Miller, Michael. *Complete Idiot's Guide to Online Search Secrets.* (2000). Indianapolis, IN: Que.

Paul, Nora, Williams, Margot, & Hane, Paula. (1999). *Great Scouts!: CyberGuides for Subject Searching on the Web.* Information Today, Inc.

Radford, Marie, Barnes, Susan, & Barr, Linda (2001). *Web Research: Selecting, Evaluating, and Citing* Boston. Allyn and Bacon.

Journal Articles

Cohen, Laura B. (1999, August). The Web as a research tool: Teaching strategies for instructors. *CHOICE Supplement 3,* 20–44.

Cohen, Laura B. (August 2000). Searching the Web: The Human Element Emerges. *CHOICE Supplement 37,* 17–31.

Introna, Lucas D., & Nissenbaum, Helen. (2000). Shaping the web: Why the politics of search engines matters. The Information Society, Vol. 16, No. 3, pp. 169–185.

Evaluating Sources on the Web

Congratulations! You've found a great Web site. Now what? The Web site you found seems like the perfect Web site for your research. But, are you sure? Why is it perfect? What criteria are you using to determine whether this Web site suits your purpose?

Think about it. Where else on earth can anyone "publish" information regardless of the *accuracy, currency,* or *reliability* of the information? The

Internet has opened up a world of opportunity for posting and distributing information and ideas to virtually everyone, even those who might post misinformation for fun, or those with ulterior motives for promoting their point of view. Armed with the information provided in this guide, you can dig through the vast amount of useless information and misinformation on the World Wide Web to uncover the valuable information. Because practically anyone can post and distribute their ideas on the Web, you need to develop a new set of *critical thinking skills* that focus on the evaluation of the quality of information, rather than be influenced and manipulated by slick graphics and flashy moving java script.

Before the existence of online sources, the validity and accuracy of a source was more easily determined. For example, in order for a book to get to the publishing stage, it must go through many critiques, validation of facts, reviews, editorial changes and the like. Ownership of the information in the book is clear because the author's name is attached to it. The publisher's reputation is on the line too. If the book turns out to have incorrect information, reputations and money can be lost. In addition, books available in a university library are further reviewed by professional librarians and selected for library purchase because of their accuracy and value to students. Journal articles downloaded or printed from online subscription services, such as Infotrac, ProQuest, EbscoHost, or other fulltext databases, are put through the same scrutiny as the paper versions of the journals.

On the World Wide Web, however, Internet service providers (ISPs) simply give Web site authors a place to store information. The Web site author can post information that may not be validated or tested for accuracy. One mistake students typically make is to assume that all information on the Web is of equal value. Also, in the rush to get assignments in on time, students may not take the extra time to make sure that the information they are citing is accurate. It is easy just to cut and paste without really thinking about the content in a critical way. However, to make sure you are gathering accurate information and to get the best grade on your assignments, it is vital that you develop your critical ability to sift through the dirt to find the diamonds.

Web Evaluation Criteria

So, here you are, at this potentially great site. Let's go though some ways you can determine if this site is one you can cite with confidence in your research. Keep in mind, ease of use of a Web site is an issue, but more important is learning how to determine the validity of data, facts, and statements for your use. The five traditional ways to verify a paper source can also be applied to your Web source: *accuracy, authority, objectivity, coverage,* and *currency.*

Evaluating Web Sites Using
Five Criteria to Judge Web Site Content

Accuracy—How reliable is the information?

Authority—Who is the author and what are his or her credentials?

Objectivity—Does the Web site present a balanced or biased point of view?

Coverage—Is the information comprehensive enough for your needs?

Currency—Is the Web site up to date?

Use additional criteria to judge Web site content, including

- **Publisher, documentation, relevance, scope, audience, appropriateness of format,** and **navigation**
- Judging whether the site is made up of **primary (original) or secondary (interpretive) sources**
- Determining whether the information is **relevant** to your research

Content Evaluation

Accuracy.   Internet searches are not the same as searches of library databases because much of the information on the Web has not been edited, whereas information in databases has. It is your responsibility to make sure that the information you use in a school project is accurate. When you examine the content on a Web site or Web page, you can ask yourself a number of questions to determine whether the information is accurate.

1. Is the information reliable?
2. Do the facts from your other research contradict the facts you find on this Web page?
3. Do any misspellings and/or grammar mistakes indicate a hastily put together Web site that has not been checked for accuracy?
4. Is the content on the page verifiable through some other source? Can you find similar facts elsewhere (journals, books, or other online sources) to support the facts you see on this Web page?
5. Do you find links to other Web sites on a similar topic? If so, check those links to ascertain whether they back up the information you see on the Web page you are interested in using.
6. Is a bibliography of additional sources for research provided? Lack of a bibliography doesn't mean the page isn't accurate, but having one allows you further investigation points to check the information.
7. Does the site of a research document or study explain how the data was collected and the type of research method used to interpret the data?

Research Navigator Guide: Special Education

If you've found a site with information that seems too good to be true, it may be. You need to verify information that you read on the Web by cross-checking against other sources.

Authority.   An important question to ask when you are evaluating a Web site is, "Who is the author of the information?" Do you know whether the author is a recognized authority in his or her field? Biographical information, references to publications, degrees, qualifications, and organizational affiliations can help to indicate an author's authority. For example, if you are researching the topic of laser surgery citing a medical doctor would be better than citing a college student who has had laser surgery.

The organization sponsoring the site can also provide clues about whether the information is fact or opinion. Examine how the information was gathered and the research method used to prepare the study or report. Other questions to ask include:

1. Who is responsible for the content of the page? Although a webmaster's name is often listed, this person is not necessarily responsible for the content.
2. Is the author recognized in the subject area? Does this person cite any other publications he or she has authored?
3. Does the author list his or her background or credentials (e.g., Ph.D. degree, title such as professor, or other honorary or social distinction)?
4. Is there a way to contact the author? Does the author provide a phone number or email address?
5. If the page is mounted by an organization, is it a known, reputable one?
6. How long has the organization been in existence?
7. Does the URL for the Web page end in the extension .edu or .org? Such extensions indicate authority compared to dotcoms (.com), which are commercial enterprises. (For example, www.cancer.com takes you to an online drugstore that has a cancer information page; www.cancer.org is the American Cancer Society Web site.)

A good idea is to ask yourself whether the author or organization presenting the information on the Web is an authority on the subject. If the answer is no, this may not be a good source of information.

Objectivity.   Every author has a point of view, and some views are more controversial than others. Journalists try to be objective by providing both sides of a story. Academics attempt to persuade readers by presenting a logical argument, which cites other scholars' work. You need to look for two sided arguments in news and information sites. For academic papers, you need to determine how the paper fits within its discipline and whether the author is using controversial methods for reporting a conclusion.

Authoritative authors situate their work within a larger discipline. This background helps readers evaluate the author's knowledge on a particular

Research Navigator Guide: Special Education

subject. You should ascertain whether the author's approach is controversial and whether he or she acknowledges this. More important, is the information being presented as fact or opinion? Authors who argue for their position provide readers with other sources that support their arguments. If no sources are cited, the material may be an opinion piece rather than an objective presentation of information. The following questions can help you determine objectivity:

1. Is the purpose of the site clearly stated, either by the author or the organization authoring the site?
2. Does the site give a balanced viewpoint or present only one side?
3. Is the information directed toward a specific group of viewers?
4. Does the site contain advertising?
5. Does the copyright belong to a person or an organization?
6. Do you see anything to indicate who is funding the site?

Everyone has a point of view. This is important to remember when you are using Web resources. A question to keep asking yourself is, What is the bias or point of *view* being expressed here?

Coverage.   Coverage deals with the breadth and depth of information presented on a Web site. Stated another way, it is about how much information is presented and how detailed the information is. Looking at the site map or index can give you an idea about how much information is contained on a site. This isn't necessarily bad. Coverage is a criteria that is tied closely to *your* research requirement. For one assignment, a given Web site may be too general for your needs. For another assignment, that same site might be perfect. Some sites contain very little actual information because pages are filled with links to other sites. Coverage also relates to objectivity You should ask the following questions about coverage:

1. Does the author present both sides of the story or is a piece of the story missing?
2. Is the information comprehensive enough for your needs?
3. Does the site cover too much, too generally?
4. Do you need more specific information than the site can provide?
5. Does the site have an objective approach?

In addition to examining what is covered on a Web site, equally revealing is what is not covered. Missing information can reveal a bias in the material. Keep in mind that you are evaluating the information on a Web site for your research requirements.

Currency.   Currency questions deal with the timeliness of information. However, currency is more important for some topics than for others. For example, currency is essential when you are looking for technology related topics and current events. In contrast, currency may not be relevant when you are doing research on Plato or Ancient Greece. In terms of Web sites, currency also pertains to whether the site is being kept up to date and links are being maintained. Sites on the Web are sometimes abandoned by their owners. When people move or change jobs, they may neglect to remove theft site from the company or university server. To test currency ask the following questions:

1. Does the site indicate when the content was created?
2. Does the site contain a last revised date? How old is the date? (In the early part of 2001, a university updated their Web site with a "last updated" date of 1901! This obviously was a Y2K problem, but it does point out the need to be observant of such things!)
3. Does the author state how often he or she revises the information? Some sites are on a monthly update cycle (e.g., a government statistics page).
4. Can you tell specifically what content was revised?
5. Is the information still useful for your topic? Even if the last update is old, the site might still be worthy of use *if* the content is still valid for your research.

Relevancy to Your Research: Primary versus Secondary Sources

Some research assignments require the use of primary (original) sources. Materials such as raw data, diaries, letters, manuscripts, and original accounts of events can be considered primary material. In most cases, these historical documents are no longer copyrighted. The Web is a great source for this type of resource.

Information that has been analyzed and previously interpreted is considered a secondary source. Sometimes secondary sources are more appropriate than primary sources. If, for example, you are asked to analyze a topic or to find an analysis of a topic, a secondary source of an analysis would be most appropriate. Ask yourself the following questions to determine whether the Web site is relevant to your research:

1. Is it a primary or secondary source?
2. Do you need a primary source?
3. Does the assignment require you to cite different types of sources? For example, are you supposed to use at least one book, one journal article, and one Web page?

You need to think critically, both visually and verbally, when evaluating Web sites. Because Web sites are designed as multimedia hypertexts, nonlinear texts, visual elements, and navigational tools are added to the evaluation process.

Help in Evaluating Web Sites.   One shortcut to finding high-quality Web sites is using subject directories and meta-sites, which select the Web sites they index by similar evaluation criteria to those just described. If you want to learn more about evaluating Web sites, many colleges and universities provide sites that help you evaluate Web resources. The following list contains some excellent examples of these evaluation sites:

- Evaluating Quality on the Net—Hope Tillman, Babson College
  www.hopetillman.com/findqual.html
- Critical Web Evaluation—Kurt W. Wagner, William Paterson University of New Jersey
  euphrates.wpunj.edu/faculty/wagnerk/
- Evalation Criteria—Susan Beck, New Mexico State University
  lib.nmsu.edu/instruction/evalcrit.html
- A Student's Guide to Research with the WWW
  www.slu.edu/departments/english/research/
- Evaluating Web Pages: Questions to Ask & Strategies for Getting the Answers
  www.lib.berkeley.edu/TeachingLib/Guides/Internet/EvalQuestions.html

Critical Evaluation Web Sites

WEB SITE AND URL	SOURCE
Critical Thinking in an Online World **www.library.ucsb.edu/untangle/ jones.html**	*Paper from "Untangling the Web" 1996*
Educom Review: Information **www.educause.edu/pub/er/review/ reviewArticles/31231.html**	*EDUCAUSE Literacy as a Liberal Art (1996 article)*
Evaluating Information Found on the Internet **MiltonsWeb.mse.jhu.edu/ research/education/net.html**	*University of Utah Library*
Evaluating Web Sites **www.lib.purdue.edu/InternetEval**	*Purdue University Library*
Evaluating Web Sites **www.lehigh.edu/~inref/guides/ evaluating.web.html**	*Lehigh University*
ICONnect: Curriculum Connections Overview **www.ala.org/ICONN/evaluate.html**	*American Library Association's technology education initiative*
Kathy Schrock's ABC's of Web Site Evaluation **www.kathyschrock.net/abceval/**	*Author's Web site*

Kids Pick the best of the Web
"Top 10: Announced"
www.ala.org/news/topkidpicks.html

*American Library Association
initiative underwritten by
Microsoft (1998)*

Resource Selection and Information
Evaluation
**alexia.lis.uiuc.edu/~janicke/
InfoAge.html**

*Univ of Illinois, Champaign-
Urbana (Librarian)*

Testing the Surf: Criteria for Evaluating
Internet Information Sources
**info.lib.uh.edu/pr/v8/n3/
smit8n3.html**

University of Houston Libraries

Evaluating Web Resources
**www2.widener.edu/
Wolfgram-Memorial-Library/
webevaluation/webeval.htm**

Widener University Library

UCLA College Library Instruction:
Thinking Critically about World
Wide Web Resources
**www.library.ucla.edu/libraries/
college/help/critical/**

UCLA Library

UG OOL: Judging Quality on the Internet
**www.open.uoguelph.ca/resources/
skills/judging.html**

University of Guelph

Web Evaluation Criteria
**lib.nmsu.edu/instruction/
evalcrit.html**

*New Mexico State University
Library*

Web Page Credibility Checklist
**www.park.pvt.k12.md.us/academics/
research/credcheck.htm**

Park School of Baltimore

Evaluating Web Sites for Educational
Uses: Bibliography and Checklist
www.unc.edu/cit/guides/irg-49.html

University of North Carolina

Evaluating Web Sites
**www.lesley.edu/library/guides/
research/evaluating_web.html**

Lesley University

> *Tip:* Can't seem to get a URL to work? If the URL doesn't begin with www,
> you may need to put the http:// in front of the URL. Usually, browsers can
> handle URLs that begin with www without the need to type in the "http://"
> but if you find you're having trouble, add the http://.

Research Navigator Guide: Special Education

Documentation Guidelines for Online Sources

Your Citation for Exemplary Research

There's another detail left for us to handle—the formal citing of electronic sources in academic papers. The very factor that makes research on the Internet exciting is the same factor that makes referencing these sources challenging: their dynamic nature. A journal article exists, either in print or on microfilm, virtually forever. A document on the Internet can come, go, and change without warning. Because the purpose of citing sources is to allow another scholar to retrace your argument, a good citation allows a reader to obtain information from your primary sources, to the extent possible. This means you need to include not only information on when a source was posted on the Internet (if available) but also when you obtained the information.

The two arbiters of form for academic and scholarly writing are the Modern Language Association (MLA) and the American Psychological Association (APA); both organizations have established styles for citing electronic publications.

MLA Style

In the fifth edition of the *MLA Handbook for Writers of Research Papers,* the MLA recommends the following formats:

- **URLs:** URLs are enclosed in angle brackets (<>) and contain the access mode identifier, the formal name for such indicators as "http" or "ftp." If a URL must be split across two lines, break it only after a slash (/). Never introduce a hyphen at the end of the first line. The URL should include all the parts necessary to identify uniquely the file/document being cited.

    <http://www.csun.edu/~rtvfdept/home/index.html>

- **An online scholarly project or reference database:** A complete "online reference contains the title of the project or database (underlined); the name of the editor of the project or database (if given); electronic publication information, including version number (if relevant and if not part of the title), date of electronic publication or latest update, and name of any sponsoring institution or organization; date of access; and electronic address.

The Perseus Project. Ed. Gregory R. Crane. Mar. 1997.
    Department of Classics, Tufts University. 15 June
    1998 <http://www.perseus.tufts.edu/>.

If you cannot find some of the information, then include the information that is available. The MLA also recommends that you print or download electronic documents, freezing them in time for future reference.

- **A document within a scholarly project or reference database:** It is much more common to use only a portion of a scholarly project or database. To cite an essay, poem, or other short work, begin this citation with the name of the author and the title of the work (in quotation marks). Then, include all the information used when citing a complete online scholarly project or reference database, however, make sure you use the URL of the specific work and not the address of the general site.

Cuthberg, Lori. "Moonwalk: Earthlings' Finest Hour."
  <u>Discovery Channel Online</u>. 1999. Discovery
  Channel. 25 Nov. 1999 <http://www.discovery.com/
  indep/newsfeatures/moonwalk/challenge.html>.

- **A professional or personal site:** Include the name of the person creating the site (reversed), followed by a period, the title of the site (underlined), or, if there is no title, a description such as Home page (such a description is neither placed in quotes nor underlined). Then, specify the name of any school, organization, or other institution affiliated with the site and follow it with your date of access and the URL of the page.

Packer, Andy. Home page. 1Apr. 1998 <http://
  www.suu.edu/~students/Packer.htm>.

Some electronic references are truly unique to the online domain. These include email, newsgroup postings, MUDs (multiuser domains) or MOOs (multiuser domains, object-oriented), and IRCs (Internet Relay Chats).

Email. In citing email messages, begin with the writer's name (reversed) followed by a period, then the title of the message (if any) in quotations as it appears in the subject line. Next comes a description of the message, typically "Email to," and the recipient (e.g., "the author"), and finally the date of the message.

Davis, Jeffrey. "Web Writing Resources." Email to
  Nora Davis. 3 Jan. 2000.

Sommers, Laurice. "Re: College Admissions
  Practices." Email to the author. 12 Aug. 1998.

List Servers and Newsgroups.   In citing these references, begin with the author's name (reversed) followed by a period. Next include the title of the document (in quotes) from the subject line, followed by the words "Online posting" (not in quotes). Follow this with the date of posting. For list servers, include the date of access, the name of the list (if known), and the online address of the list's moderator or administrator. For newsgroups, follow "Online posting" with the date of posting, the date of access, and the name of the newsgroup, prefixed with "news:" and enclosed in angle brackets.

Applebaum, Dale. "Educational Variables." Online
    posting. 29 Jan. 1998. Higher Education
    Discussion Group. 30 Jan. 1993
    <jlucidoj@unc.edu>.

Gostl, Jack. "Re: Mr. Levitan." Online posting.
    13 June 1997. 20 June 1997
    <news:alt.edu.bronxscience>.

MUDs, MOOs, and IRCs.   Begin with the name of the speaker(s) followed by a period. Follow with the description and date of the event, the forum in which the communication took place, the date of access, and the online address. If you accessed the MOO or MUD through telnet, your citation might appear as follows:

Guest. Personal interview. 13 Aug. 1998.
    <telnet://du.edu:8888>.

For more information on MLA documentation style for online sources, check out their Web site at http://www.mla.org/style/sources.htm.

APA Style

The newly revised *Publication Manual of the American Psychological Association* (5th ed.) now includes guidelines for Internet resources. The manual recommends that, at a minimum, a reference of an Internet source should provide a document title or description, a date (either the date of publication or update or the date of retrieval), and an address (in Internet terms, a uniform resource locator, or URL). Whenever possible, identify the authors of a document as well. It's important to remember that, unlike the MLA, the APA does not include temporary or transient sources (e.g., letters, phone calls, etc.) in its "References" page, preferring to handle them in the text. The general suggested format is as follows:

Online periodical:

Author, A. A., Author, B. B., & Author, C. C.
  (2000). Title of article. *Title of Periodical,*
  xx, xxxxx. Retrieved month, day, year, from
  source.

Online document:

Author, A. A. (2000). *Title of work.* Retrieved
  month, day, year, from source.

Some more specific examples are as follows:

FTP (File Transfer Protocol) Sites.   To cite files available for downloading via FTP, give the author's name (if known), the publication date (if
available and if different from the date accessed), the full title of the paper
(capitalizing only the first word and proper nouns), the date of access, and
the address of the FTP site along with the full path necessary to access the
file.

Deutsch, P. (1991) Archie: An electronic directory
  service for the Internet. Retrieved January 25,
  2000 from File Transfer Protocol: ftp://
  ftp.sura.net/pub/archie/docs/whatis.archie

WWW Sites (World Wide Web).   To cite files available for viewing or
downloading via the World Wide Web, give the author's name (if known),
the year of publication (if known and if different from the date accessed),
the full title of the article, and the title of the complete work (if applicable)
in italics. Include any additional information (such as versions, editions, or
revisions) in parentheses immediately following the title. Include the date
of retrieval and full URL (the http address).

Burka, L. P. (1993). A hypertext history of multiuser dungeons. *MUDdex.* Retrieved January 13, 1997
  from the World Wide Web: http://www.utopia.com/
  talent/lpb/muddex/essay/

Tilton, J. (1995). Composing good HTML (Vers. 2.0.6).
  Retrieved December 1, 1996 from the World Wide Web:
  http://www.cs.cmu.edu/~tilt/cgh/

Synchronous Communications (MOOs, MUDs, IRC, etc.).   Give the
name of the speaker(s), the complete date of the conversation being ref-
erenced in parentheses, and the title of the session (if applicable). Next,

list the title of the site in italics, the protocol and address (if applicable), and any directions necessary to access the work. Last, list the date of access, followed by the retrieval information. Personal interviews do not need to be listed in the References, but do need to be included in parenthetic references in the text (see the APA *Publication Manual*).

Cross, J. (1996, February 27). Netoric's Tuesday "cafe: Why use MUDs in the writing classroom? *MediaMoo*. Retrieved March 1, 1996 from File Transfer Protocol: ftp://daedalus.com/ pub/ACW/NETORIC/catalog

Gopher Sites.   List the author's name (if applicable), the year of publication, the title of the file or paper, and the title of the complete work (if applicable). Include any print publication information (if available) followed by the protocol (i.e., gopher://). List the date that the file was accessed and the path necessary to access the file.

Massachusetts Higher Education Coordinating Council. (1994). Using coordination and collaboration to address change. Retrieved July 16, 1999 from the World Wide Web: gopher://gopher.mass.edu:170/ 00gopher_root%3A%5B_hecc%5D_plan

Email, Listservs, and Newsgroups.   Do not include personal email in the list of References. Although unretrievable communication such as email is not included in APA References, somewhat more public or accessible Internet postings from newsgroups or listservs may be included. See the APA *Publication Manual* for information on in-text citations.

Heilke, J. (1996, May 3). Webfolios. Alliance for Computers and Writing Discussion List. Retrieved December 31, 1996 from the World Wide Web: http://www.ttu.edu/lists/acw-1/9605/0040.html

Other authors and educators have proposed similar extensions to the APA style. You can find links to these pages at:

www.psychwww.com/resource/apacrib.htm

Remember, "frequently-referenced" does not equate to "correct" "or even "desirable." Check with your professor to see if your course or school has a preference for an extended APA style.

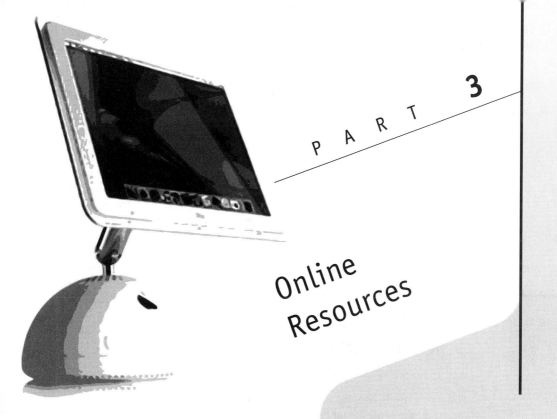

P A R T 3

Online
Resources

Internet Sites Useful in Special Education

Part 2 of this guide contains information designed to help teachers and prospective teachers use the Internet and the World Wide Web in their work with students with exceptionalities. My intention is to provide basic information needed by special and general educators as well as useful and interesting resources. Here you will find information on disabilities included under federal special education law as well as the laws themselves. You'll also learn where to locate some of the technical assistance available on the Web, from writing individualized education plans and behavior change plans to adapting lessons and materials for students who are disabled or gifted in regular education classrooms. In addition, you'll find information on working with families, as well as individuals.

The Web sites in this guide have been selected to be representative of the best the Web has to offer. For the most part, national organizations and comprehensive Web sites are highlighted rather than isolated local or regional pages, although occasionally I have included a site simply because of the interesting or hard-to-find information it provides. I have tried to stay away from sites that were created purely for the purpose of selling a product or a particular agenda. My hope is that this information will expand your knowledge base, enrich your teaching, and help you discover the possibilities of the Web.

Why Are the Internet and the World Wide Web Important for Special Education?

A major advantage of the Internet is that it provides a connection to other people. In addition to email, the Internet provides an opportunity to use chat rooms and newsgroups to talk to and ask questions of all stakeholders (people who are disabled, parents, and professionals) in the education of students with disabilities. We Media is a great place to start. Similar to Yahoo, Excite, and other Internet portals (i.e., launching points), it is an integrated on-line community created by and for people with disabilities, their families and friends. It also provides access to a talking Web browser for people with low vision or learning disabilities and a free subscription to WeMedia magazine, a consumer lifestyle publication that has won critical acclaim for its editorial content and innovative approach to cross-disability issues.

We Media: The Disability Network

http://www.wemedia.com

Today's schools contain increasing numbers of children who have disabilities that were previously unheard of or considered rare. There are many resources on various disabilities/syndromes that previously would have

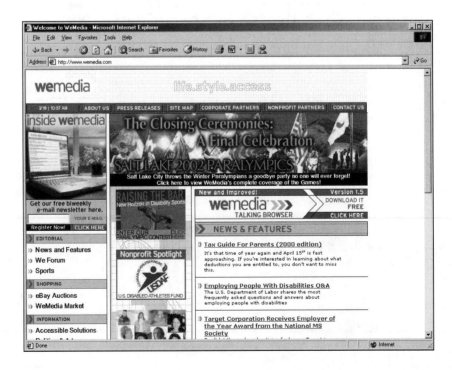

been difficult, if not impossible to locate. For example, where could you find information if someone asked you about hyperlexia, Rett syndrome, Angelman syndrome, or Williams syndrome? Chances are that you wouldn't be able to find the information by pulling a book off the shelf or even spending hours in the library. However, with a few clicks of the mouse, not only can you find in-depth information on the characteristics, identification, and treatment of various disabilities, but you can also link to support groups for families. The following Web sites are examples of this type of information. Later sections of this guide provide information on the 13 categories of disability under federal special education law as well as resources related to giftedness.

American Hyperlexia Association

`http://www.hyperlexia.org`

This Web site provides information on hyperlexia, which is a syndrome on the autism spectrum characterized by a precocious ability to read words, significant difficulty in understanding verbal language, and difficulty in socializing and interacting appropriately with people.

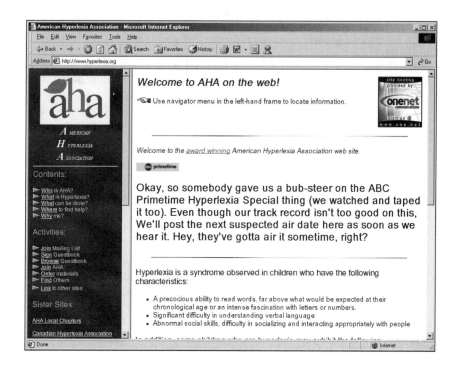

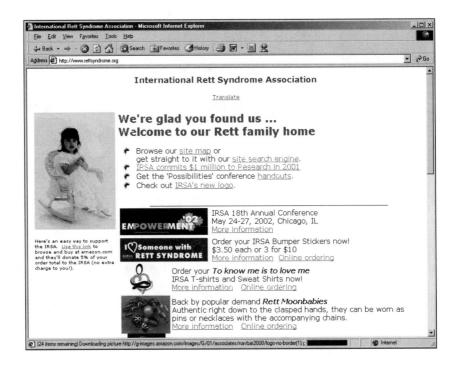

International Rett Syndrome Association

`http://www.rettsyndrome.org`

Rett syndrome is a disorder that affects females and is often misdiagnosed as autism, cerebral palsy, or non-specific developmental delay. A child with Rett syndrome usually begins life with apparently normal or near normal development until 6-18 months then loses communication skills and purposeful use of the hands, followed by stereotyped hand movements, gait disturbances, and slowing of the rate of head growth as well as scoliosis.

Angelman Syndrome Foundation

`http://www.angelman.org`

Angelman syndrome is characterized by severe developmental delay, speech impairment, a movement or balance disorder, and behavioral symptoms including any combination of frequent laughter/smiling; apparent happy demeanor; easily excitable personality, often with hand flapping movements; hypermotoric behavior; short attention span.

Williams Syndrome Association

`http://www.williams-syndrome.org`

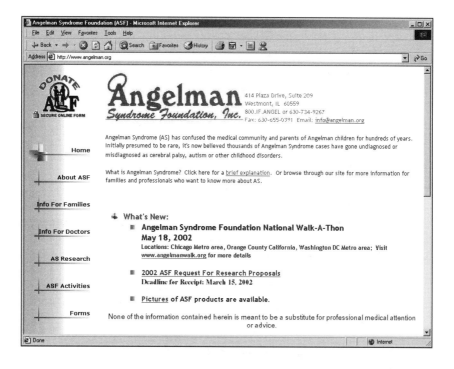

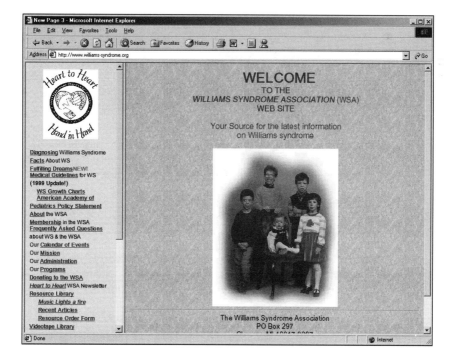

Williams syndrome is a rare genetic condition that causes medical and developmental problems. Common symptoms include a characteristic facial appearance, cardiovascular and musculoskeletal disorders, sensitive hearing, smallness in stature, an overly friendly personality, and intellectual problems such as developmental delay, learning disability, or attention deficit disorder.

There are many library resources available on the Internet. University libraries frequently provide enrolled students access to the full text of scholarly articles on line. Visit your university's Web site and see what it has to offer.

Other Web sites contain databases that enable you to find scholarly articles, as well as updates on the latest research and promising practices. For example, the ERIC (Educational Resources Information Center) system is a nationwide information network of 16 federally funded clearinghouses. The ERIC Clearinghouse on Disabilities and Gifted Education (ERIC EC) gathers and disseminates professional literature, information, and resources via databases, fact sheets, frequently asked questions (FAQs), and mini-bibliographies. The ERIC EC database contains more than 70,000 citations on disabilities or gifted topics.

The Educational Resources Information Center

http://www.eric.ed.gov

ERIC Clearinghouse on Disabilities and Gifted Education

http://ericec.org

Special Education Terminology

Confused by the alphabet soup of disability-related terms on documents and reports? Here are some quick guides to some of the more common acronyms in disability education, law, medicine, and rehabilitation.

Alphabet Soup: Disability Related Acronyms

http://www.disabilityresources.org/ABC.html

Glossary of Special Ed Terms

http://www.disabilityrights.org/glossary.htm

Special Education Glossary

http://specialed.peoriaud.k12.az.us/spdgloss.htm

Research Navigator Guide: Special Education

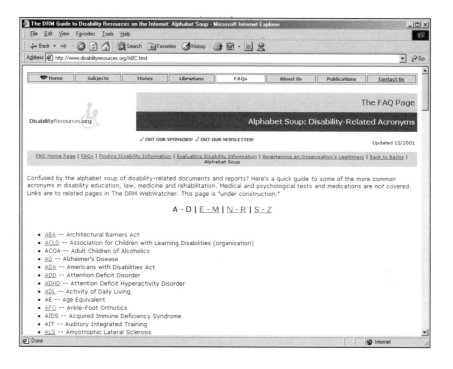

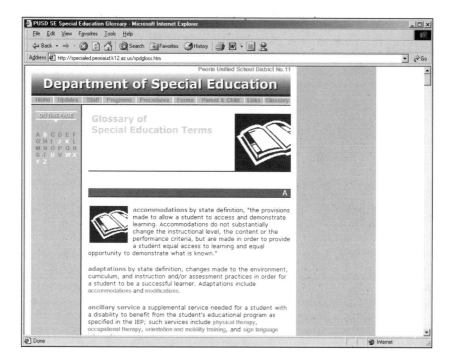

The Internet as a Tool for Your Studies in Special Education

Using the Internet, you can expand your knowledge base about the historical context and legal basis for special education. You can obtain information on current laws, regulations, and court cases that enable the teacher to understand both the letter and the spirit of the law. You can also learn how to use non-labeling, people-first language or provide this information to others.

HISTORICAL AND PHILOSOPHICAL BACKGROUND OF SPECIAL EDUCATION

Special Education as an Outgrowth of the Civil Rights Movement. Historically, people with disabilities have been excluded from society. The biggest advances in civil rights came as an outgrowth of the civil rights movements of the 1960s. As African Americans, women, and other social minorities gained political influence, so, too, did people with disabilities. Public Law 94-142, the first comprehensive federal special education law, was passed in 1975. However, it was not until 1990 and the passage of the Americans with Disabilities Act, which contains wording similar to the Civil Rights Act of 1964 and Section 504 of the Vocational Rehabilitation Act of 1973, that people with disabilities won the legal right to freedom from discrimination.

Disability Rights Movement Virtual Exhibition

http://www.americanhistory.si.edu/disabilityrights/welcome.html

A virtual exhibition created by the Smithsonian National Museum of American History

Disability Social History Project

http://www.disabilityhistory.org/dshp.html

A timeline provides significant dates and other important information about the history of people with disabilities and special education.

Non-Labeling Language. The language we use when referring to people with disabilities can either convey respect and dignity, or it can demean or dishonor them. Special educators should avoid using language that has negative connotations and evokes pity or fear. Learn why language can make a difference and how to use it appropriately.

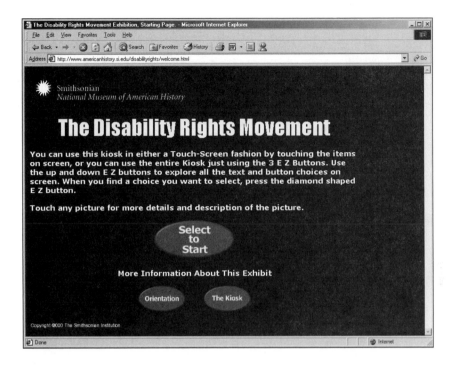

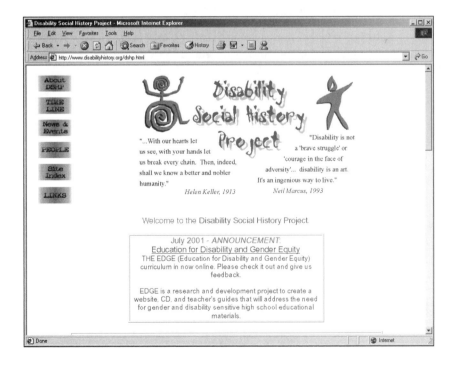

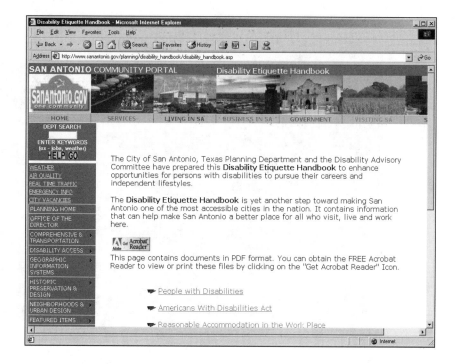

Disability Etiquette Handbook

```
http://www.sanantonio.gov/planning/
disability_handbook/disability_handbook.asp
```

People First Language

```
http://www.kidstogether.org/pep-1st.htm
```

Words with Dignity

```
http://www.paraquad.org/wwd.htm
```

The Special Educator as Advocate. In its Code of Ethics and Standards of Practice, The Council for Exceptional Children has clearly stated that educators should "serve as advocates for exceptional students by speaking, writing, and acting in a variety of situations on their behalf."

Code of Ethics and Standards of Practice for Educators of Persons with Exceptionalities

```
http://www.cec.sped.org/ps/code.html#1
```

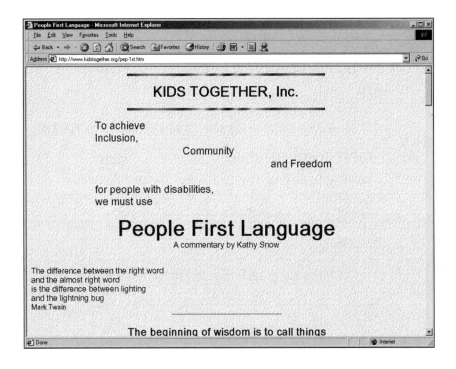

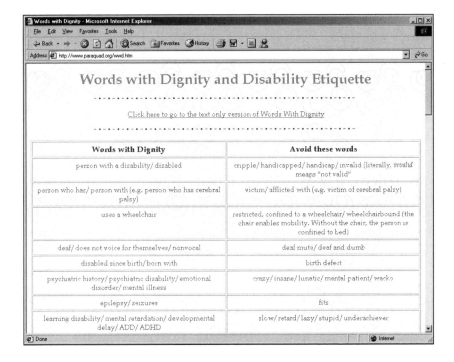

The following Web sites provide information for people interested in working for the rights of people with disabilities.

The Disability Rights Activist

`http://disrights.org`

Disability Rights Education and Defense Fund (DREDF)

`http://www.dredf.org`

DREDF is a national law and policy center dedicated to protecting and advancing the civil rights of people with disabilities through legislation, litigation, advocacy, technical assistance, and education and training of attorneys, advocates, persons with disabilities, and parents of children with disabilities.

The National Association of Protection and Advocacy Systems

`http://protectionandadvocacy.com`

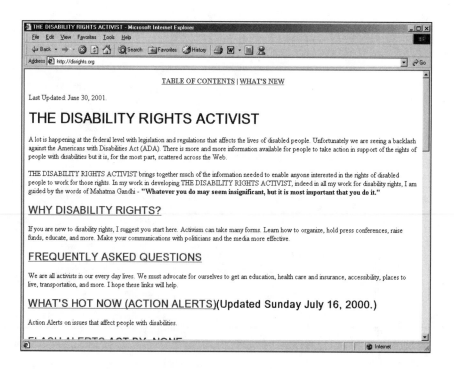

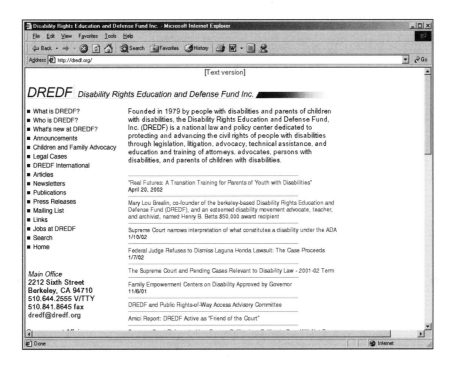

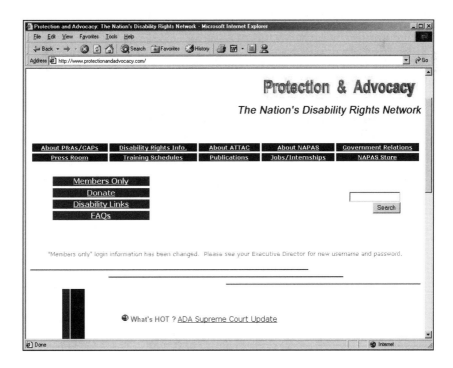

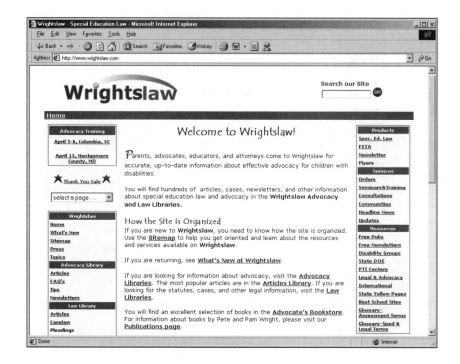

Research Navigator Guide: Special Education

Wrightslaw: The Special Ed Advocate

`http://www.wrightslaw.com`

Subscribe to The Special Ed Advocate, a free online newsletter about special education law, advocacy, research, and other topics.

LEGAL ASPECTS OF EDUCATING STUDENTS WITH EXCEPTIONALITIES

The Individuals with Disabilities Education Act (IDEA).   The IDEA is the federal special education law. Originally passed in 1975 as the Education of All Handicapped Children Act (P.L. 94-142), the 1997 Amendments and the federal regulations that implement the law are available on many Web sites. One of the most comprehensive sites, Idea Practices, answers your questions about the Individuals with Disabilities Education Act. It contains a hyper-linked version of the federal regulations by section and subject area as well as Department of Education updates, the annual report to Congress on implementation of the IDEA, and other law-related resources. Resources include strategies and teaching methods for specific disabilities and situations, as well as case studies from schools implementing promising practices.

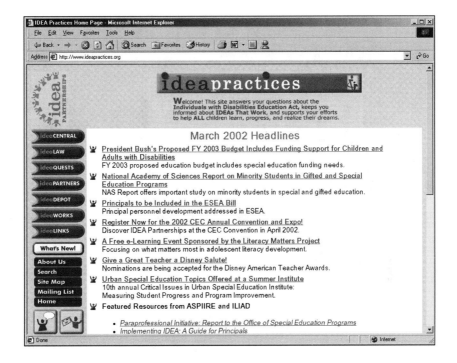

Idea Practices

http://www.ideapractices.org

IDEA '97

http://www.ed.gov/offices/OSERS/IDEA/index.html

Section 504 of the Vocational Rehabilitation Act. Section 504 prohibits discrimination on the basis of disability in federally funded programs. In schools that receive any kind of federal funding, all students with disabilities are entitled to reasonable accommodations under Section 504, whether or not they receive special education services.

Office for Civil Rights Fact Sheet: Your Rights Under Section 504

http://www.os.dhhs.gov/ocr/504.html

A Parent and Educator's Guide to Section 504

http://www.pathfinder.minot.com/section504.html

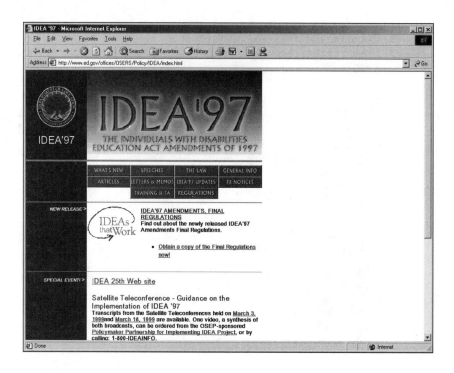

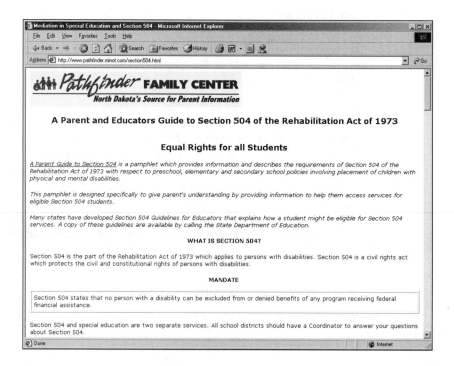

Section 504: A Resource Guide from Jefferson County (Colorado) Public Schools

`http://204.98.1.2/isu/504`

The Americans with Disabilities Act (ADA).   The ADA is wide ranging legislation that prohibits discrimination against people with disabilities in the areas of employment, public services and accommodations, and telecommunications. It is intended to make American society more accessible for people with disabilities.

Americans with Disabilities Act Document Center

`http://janweb.icdi.wvu.edu/kinder/index.htm`

U.S. Department of Justice ADA Home Page

`http://www.usdoj.gov/crt/ada/adahom1.htm`

Do you have trouble understanding the basic provisions of these laws? Wondering how to explain them to parents or other teachers? The following Web sites provide comparisons among the three laws:

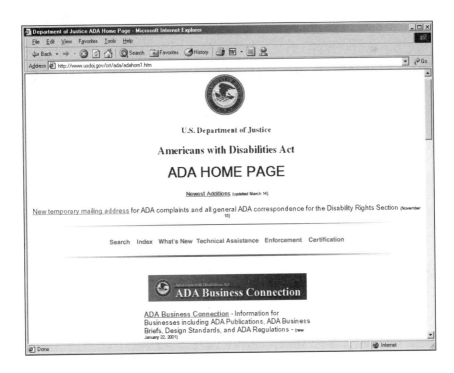

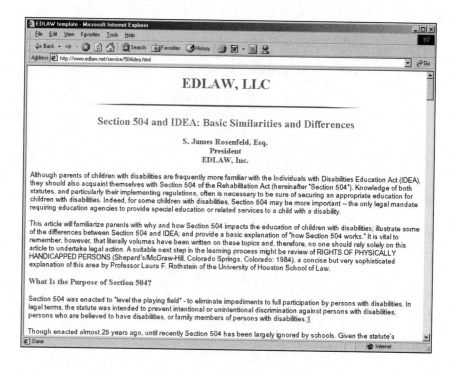

Section 504 and IDEA: Basic Similarities and Differences

http://www.edlaw.net/service/504idea.html

Comparative Analysis: IDEA, Section 504 and the ADA

http://www.spedalliance.com/
comparative_analysis.htm

Government. The U.S. Department of Education's Office of Special Education and Rehabilitative Services (OSERS) is the branch of the government that supports special education programs for individuals from birth through 21, provides rehabilitation of youth and adults with disabilities, and supports research.

Office of Special Education and Rehabilitative Services

http://www.ed.gov/offices/OSERS

The OSERS Web site links to each of its three branches.

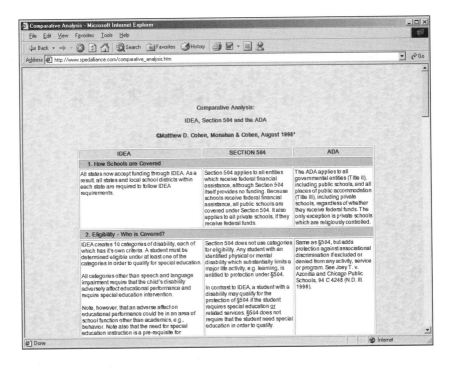

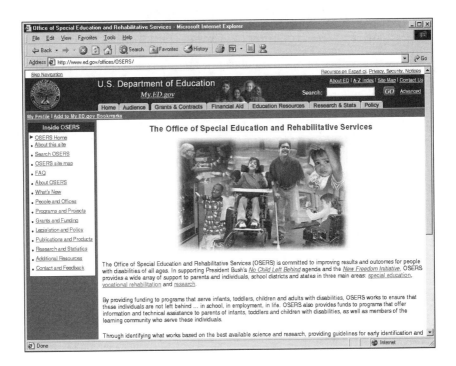

Office of Special Education Programs

`http://www.ed.gov/offices/OSERS/OSEP/index.html`

The Office of Special Education Programs is responsible for administering programs and projects relating to the free appropriate public education of all children, youth and adults with disabilities, from birth through age 21. The Web site for this agency contains the latest news regarding special education programs and many resources for teachers, including training materials related to the IDEA, copies of reports on topics such as preventing school violence, funding information, and a searchable database of projects.

The Rehabilitation Services Administration

`http://www.ed.gov/offices/OSERS/RSA/index.html`

The Rehabilitation Services Administration develops and implements comprehensive and coordinated programs of vocational rehabilitation, supported employment, and independent living for individuals with disabilities, through services, training, research and economic opportunities, in order to maximize their employability, independence, and integration into the workplace and the community.

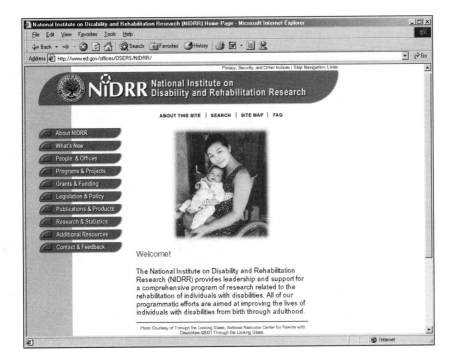

The National Institute on Disability and Rehabilitation Research

`http://www.ed.gov/offices/OSERS/NIDRR`

The National Institute on Disability and Rehabilitation Research conducts comprehensive and coordinated programs of research and related activities to maximize the full inclusion, social integration, employment, and independent living of disabled individuals of all ages.

The Supreme Court.   Information about special education and the Supreme Court can be found at the following Web sites.

The Cornell University Law Library

`http://supct.law.cornell.edu/supct`

The Supreme Court Collection from the Legal Information Institute at Cornell University presents Supreme Court decisions and a variety of information about the Supreme Court, including a glossary of legal terms.

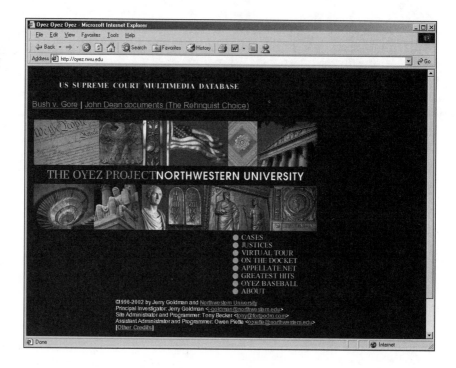

The Oyez Project

`http://oyez.nwu.edu`

The Oyez Project is a collection of multimedia files related to the U.S. Supreme Court. You can hear streaming audio clips of oral arguments and read written opinions from many Supreme Court cases. The site also features a virtual tour of the Supreme Court building and biographies and photos of justices.

DOCUMENTING ELECTRONIC SOURCES IN YOUR SCHOLARLY WRITING

The American Psychological Association's (APA) style of writing is the preferred format for educators in the field of special education. You can find online assistance in writing papers for coursework or submission for publication.

APA Style Resources

`http://www.psychwww.com/resource/apacrib.htm`

This Web site contains a list of links to resources on using APA style.

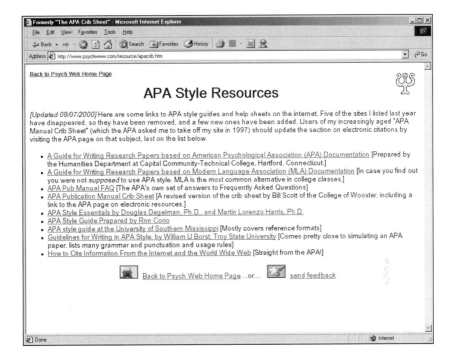

Research Navigator Guide: Special Education

Electronic Reference Formats Recommended by the APA

http://www.apastyle.org/elccref.html

The American Psychological Association has created a Web site to assist authors in documenting online sources. The APA approved this extension of the APA manual in 1999.

A Guide for Writing Research Papers Based on Styles Recommended by the APA

http://webster.commnet.edu/apa/apa_index.htm

The Humanities Department and library staff at Capital Community College in Hartford, Connecticut use a question and answer format to present information on APA style.

INFORMATION ON SPECIFIC DISABILITIES UNDER FEDERAL SPECIAL EDUCATION LAW

In order for students to receive special education services under the Individuals with Disabilities Education Act, a multidisciplinary team must determine that they have at least one of the following disabilities and that

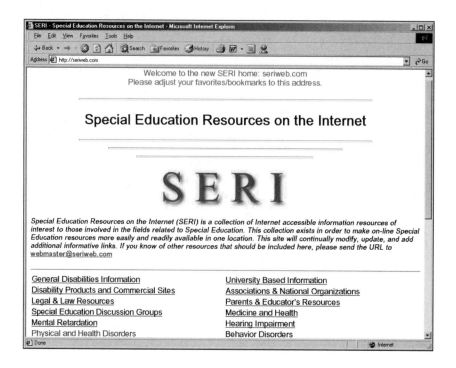

they need specially designed instruction. First, though, visit a "super site" which contains information on many categories of disability as well as specific resources for parent, teachers, and information on topics such as inclusion, transition, and products for people with disabilities, their families and teachers.

Special Education Resources on the Internet (SERI)

http://seriweb.com

The following sections provide resource information on the categories of disability under the IDEA. For each category, a summary of the federal definition under the IDEA (Section 300.7, Child with a Disability) is provided.

AUTISM

Autism is a developmental disability that significantly affects verbal and nonverbal communication and social interaction. Characteristics often associated with autism are engagement in repetitive activities and stereotyped movements, resistance to environmental change or change in daily routines, and unusual responses to sensory experiences.

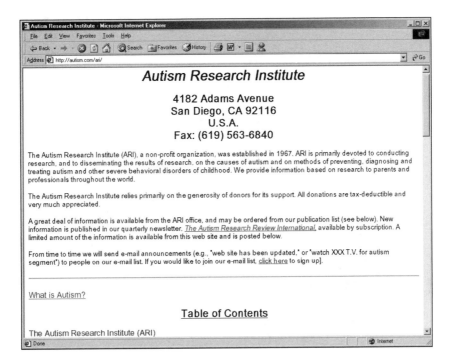

Autism Research Institute (ARI)

`http://www.autism.com/ari`

ARI is primarily devoted to conducting research, and to disseminating the results of research to parents and professionals, on the causes of autism and methods of preventing, diagnosing and treating autism.

Autism Society of America (ASA)

`http://www.autism-society.org`

The ASA provides information and resources for professionals and families of individuals with autism. The "Getting Started" section provides basic information on autism and treatment approaches.

Center for the Study of Autism

`http://www.autism.org`

Subgroups, issues, interventions, overview in different languages

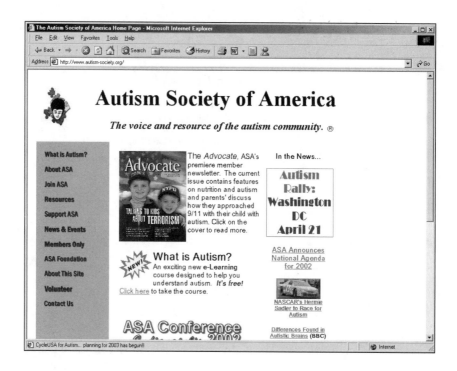

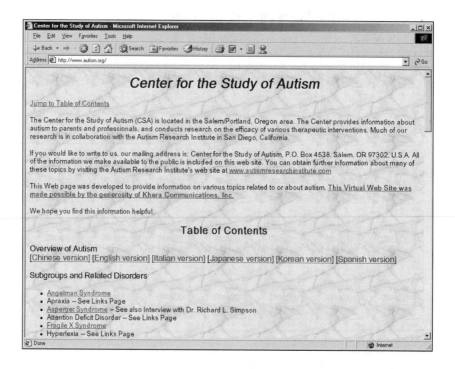

Ooops. . . . Wrong Planet Syndrome

`http://www.isn.net/~jypsy`

The mother of a boy with autism created this award-winning site. It contains definitions of autism and related disorders and an extensive list of resources and links to other sites ("more links than you can shake a stick at"), as well as mail lists, forums, chat rooms, and newsgroups.

DEAF–BLINDNESS

A student with deaf–blindness has both hearing and visual impairments, the combination of which causes such severe communication and other developmental and educational needs that they cannot be accommodated in special education programs solely for children with deafness or children with blindness.

A–Z to Deaf–Blindness

`http://www.deafblind.com`

This site, created by a man who is deaf and blind, contains information about deaf–blindness, including the deaf–blind manual alphabet. Did you know that a person with a red and white cane is deaf–blind?

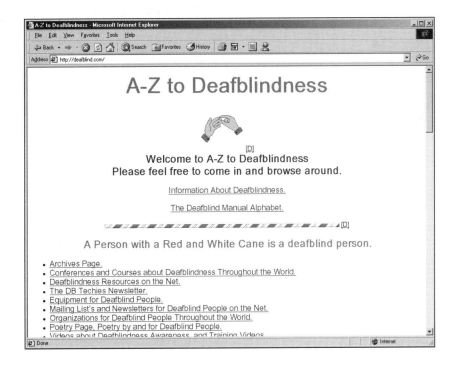

Research Navigator Guide: Special Education

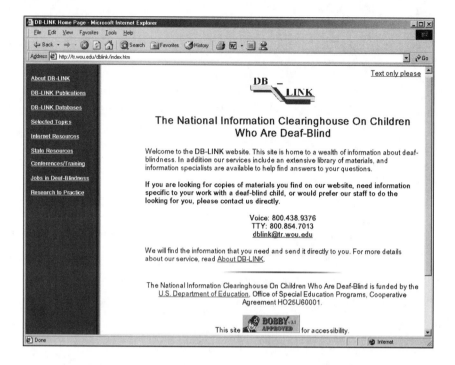

D-B Link: National Information Clearinghouse for Children who are Deaf–Blind

http://www.tr.wou.edu/dblink/index.htm

Databases, publications, many useful links.

Helen Keller National Center for Deaf-Blind Youths and Adults

http://www.helenkeller.org/national/index.htm

Comprehensive information on vocational and personal adjustment training, links to resources and technical assistance to educators.

DEAFNESS

Deafness means a hearing impairment that is so severe that the child is impaired in processing linguistic information through hearing, with or without amplification.

Alexander Graham Bell Association for the Deaf (AGBell)

http://www.agbell.org

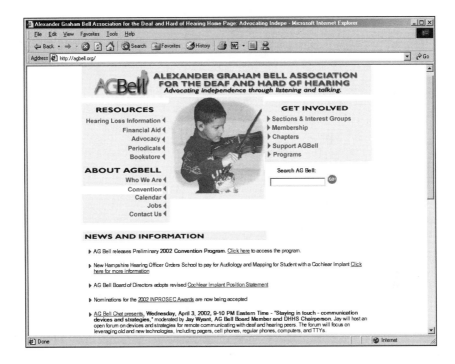

The Alexander Graham Bell Association for the Deaf and Hard of Hearing (AG Bell) is an international organization comprised of parents, adults with hearing loss, and professionals who serve children with hearing loss. AG Bell was founded in 1890 by Alexander Graham Bell as an information provider and support network. AG Bell is the largest organization in the U.S. focused on the needs of hearing impaired children who use auditory approaches to communicate.

Council on Education of the Deaf

`http://www.deafed.net`

Curriculum materials, instructional strategies, job board, teacher preparation programs.

Wallace Library Guides

`http://wally.rit.edu/internet/subject/deafness.html`

Links to an extensive set of resources for people who are deaf or hard of hearing, including several interactive Web-based American Sign Language and finger spelling sites.

EMOTIONAL DISTURBANCE

A student with emotional disturbance exhibits one or more of the following characteristics over a long period of time and to a marked degree:

- An inability to learn that cannot be explained by intellectual, sensory, or health factors;
- An inability to build or maintain satisfactory interpersonal relationships with peers and teachers;
- Inappropriate types of behavior or feelings under normal circumstances;
- A general pervasive mood of unhappiness or depression
- A tendency to develop physical symptoms or fears associated with personal or school problems.

The term does not apply to children who are socially maladjusted, or have inappropriate behaviors, unless it is determined that they have an emotional disturbance.

American Academy of Child and Adolescent Psychiatry

`http://www.aacap.org`

The stated purpose of this site is to assist "parents and families in understanding developmental, behavioral, emotional and mental disorders af-

fecting children and adolescents." Teachers will benefit from its straight-forward fact sheets on a variety of topics, as well as information on the nature of child and adolescent psychiatry. The glossary provides information on alcohol and drug abuse, anorexia nervosa, anxiety, attention deficit hyperactivity disorder, bipolar disorder (manic-depression), bulimia nervosa, conduct disorder, depression, obsessive-compulsive disorder, physical abuse, post-traumatic stress disorder, psychosis, schizophrenia, sexual abuse, suicide, and Tourette's syndrome.

Center for Effective Collaboration and Practice (CECP)

`http://cecp.air.org/index.htm`

CECP promotes collaboration among Federal agencies serving children with or at risk of developing emotional disabilities. This site includes Federal Resources, online resources, including articles, reports, monographs, mini-Web sites, statistics and email listservs, and many links to resources on issues of emotional and behavioral problems in children and youth.

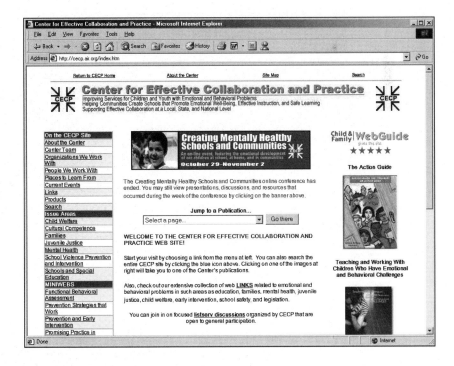

Research Navigator Guide: Special Education

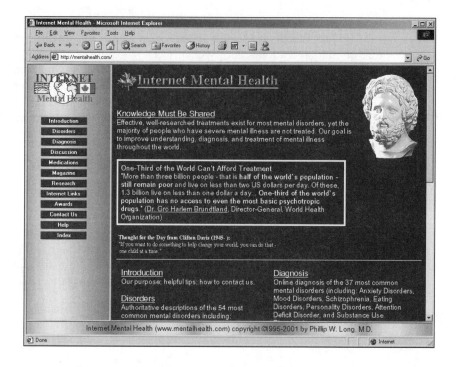

Internet Mental Health

`http://www.mentalhealth.com`

This Web site is a virtual encyclopedia of mental health information. It contains descriptions, diagnosis, treatment, medications, and research for 54 mental disorders; in-depth information about the 72 most commonly prescribed drugs; and, an online magazine.

National Association for the Mentally Ill

`http://www.nami.org`

News, research, resources, helpline, books, topical information.

HEARING IMPAIRMENT

Hearing impairment means an impairment in hearing, whether permanent or fluctuating, that adversely affects a child's educational performance but that is not included under the definition of deafness.

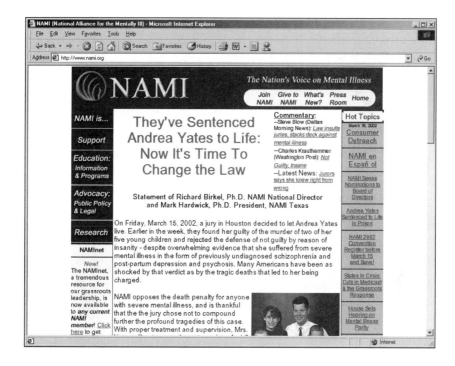

Alexander Graham Bell Association for the Deaf and Hard of Hearing

`http://www.agbell.org`

This organization focuses on the needs of children with hearing impairments who use auditory approaches to communicate.

Hard of Hearing and Deaf Students: A Resource Guide to Support Classroom Teachers

`http://www.bced.gov.bc.ca/specialed/hearimpair/toc.htm`

This site, sponsored by the British Columbia Ministry of Education, provides information for teachers on hearing loss, preparing to teach children with hearing impairments, tips on classroom adaptation and communication.

MENTAL RETARDATION

Mental retardation means significantly subaverage general intellectual functioning, existing concurrently with deficits in adaptive behavior and manifested during the developmental period.

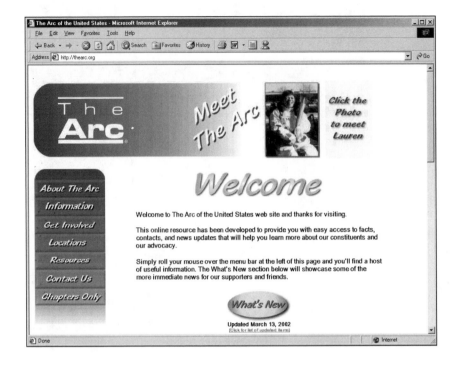

The Arc of the United States

http://thearc.org

The Arc is a national advocacy organization for people with mental retardation and related disabilities and their families. You can shop on line for informational materials about mental retardation and related developmental disabilities, and many of these materials are free. In addition to many links, this site provides access to information on the Americans with Disabilities Act, criminal justice, fetal alcohol syndrome, and the human genome project. You can participate in discussions and view the Capitol Insider, a weekly bulletin on what is happening on Capitol Hill.

National Down Syndrome Association

http://www.ndss.org

The NDSS Web site bills itself as a comprehensive, online information source about Down syndrome. One very useful feature for college students is a page created just to help students do research on Down syndrome.

National Fragile X Foundation

http://www.nfxf.org

Fragile-X Syndrome is the most common form of genetic inherited mental retardation. The foundation provides information, support, consultation and referrals, as well as a newsletter.

MULTIPLE DISABILITIES

Multiple disabilities means impairments that occur at the same time (such as mental retardation-blindness, mental retardation-orthopedic impairment, etc.), the combination of which causes such severe educational needs that they cannot be accommodated in special education programs solely for one of the impairments. The term does not include deaf-blindness.

Activity Ideas for Students with Severe/Profound/Multiple Disabilities

http://www.palaestra.com/featurestory.html

A feature article by PALAESTRA (Forum of Sport, Physical Education, and Recreation for People with Disabilities) presents six units of activities that could easily be carried out by teachers.

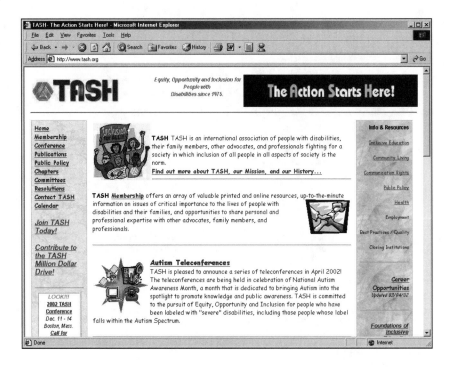

The Association for Persons with Severe Disabilities

http://www.tash.org

Conferences, newsletter, discussion groups, grassroots advocacy.

ORTHOPEDIC IMPAIRMENT

The federal definition of orthopedic impairment merely lists example of disabilities that are considered orthopedic impairments. An orthopedic impairment is a motor disability caused by an anomaly, disease, or other condition (for example, cerebral palsy, spina bifida, muscular dystrophy, or traumatic injury) where the child requires specialized and integrated services in order to benefit from an educational program.

Information about Mobility Impairments

http://spot.pcc.edu/osd/mobinfo.htm

Muscular Dystrophy Association

http://www.mdausa.org

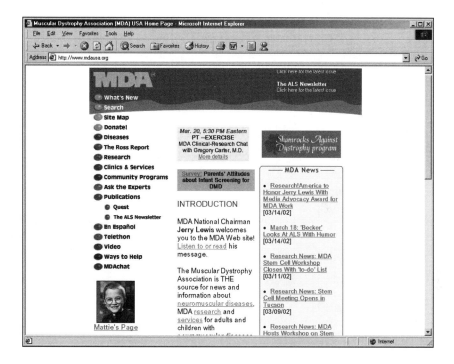

A comprehensive guide to materials about 40 different neuromuscular diseases, plus information about the usual age of onset and characteristics of each disorder.

Strategies for Teaching Children with Motor/Orthopedic Impairments

http://www.as.wvu.edu/~scidis/motor.html

United Cerebral Palsy Association

http://www.ucpa.org

United Cerebral Palsy's mission is to advance the independence, productivity and full citizenship of people with cerebral palsy and other disabilities, through a commitment to independence, inclusion, and self-determination. The Web site provides information on advocacy initiatives, links to national resources and information, and much more.

Research Navigator Guide: Special Education

OTHER HEALTH IMPAIRMENT INCLUDING ATTENTION DEFICIT DISORDER

Other health impairment means having limited strength, vitality or alertness, including a heightened alertness to environmental stimuli, that results in limited alertness with respect to the educational environment. The impairment is due to chronic or acute health problems such as asthma, attention deficit disorder or attention deficit hyper activity disorder, diabetes, epilepsy, a heart condition, hemophilia, lead poisoning, leukemia, nephritis, rheumatic fever, and sickle cell anemia.

Band-aides and Blackboards: When Chronic Illness or Some Other Medical Problem Goes to School

`http://www.faculty.fairfield.edu/fleitas/contents.html`

Tons of information for children, teens, and adults, including tips for teachers, nurses, doctors, and parents.

CHADD

`http://www.chadd.org`

Children and Adults with Attention Deficit Disorder support group and information/resources.

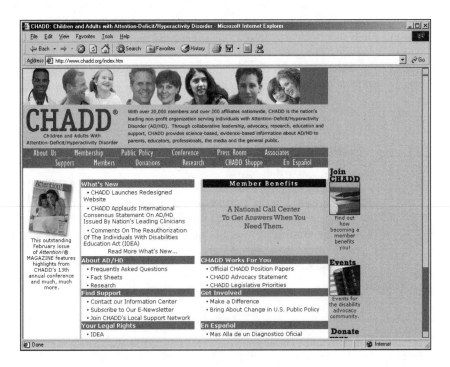

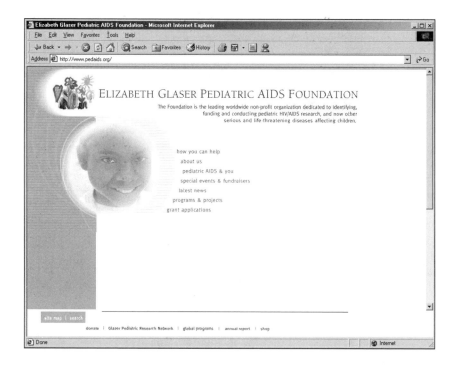

Elizabeth Glaser Pediatric AIDS Foundation

http://www.pedaids.org

A worldwide nonprofit organization dedicated to identifying, funding, and conducting AIDS/HIV research.

The Epilepsy Foundation

http://www.efa.org

The Epilepsy Foundation (formerly the Epilepsy Foundation of America) is a national organization that works for people affected by seizures through research, education, advocacy, and service. A section of this Web site is devoted to information for teachers.

National Attention Deficit Disorder Association

http://www.add.org

This site is about research, treatment, and family and legal issues pertaining to ADD and ADHD. It features personal stories and has Kid's Area in which children are encouraged to provide their opinions and thoughts about the disorders. Also contains links to support groups and other Web sites.

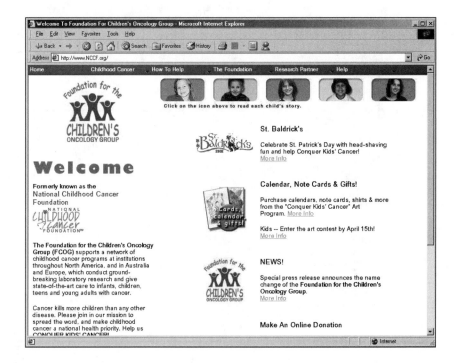

Foundation for the Children's Oncology Group

`http://www.nccf.org`

This organization supports a network of childhood cancer treatment and research institutions throughout North America. The Web site provides information and resources for people connected to childhood cancer patients.

National Organization for Rare Disorders (NORD)

`http://www.rarediseases.org`

NORD is a unique federation of more than 140 not-for-profit voluntary health organizations serving people with rare disorders and disabilities. A rare or "orphan" disease affects fewer than 200,000 people in the United States. There are more than 6,000 rare disorders that, taken together, affect approximately 25 million Americans. NORD serves as a clearinghouse for information on rare disorders and provides referrals to additional sources of assistance and ongoing support.

SPECIFIC LEARNING DISABILITY

A learning disability is disorder in one or more of the basic psychological processes involved in understanding or in using spoken or written lan-

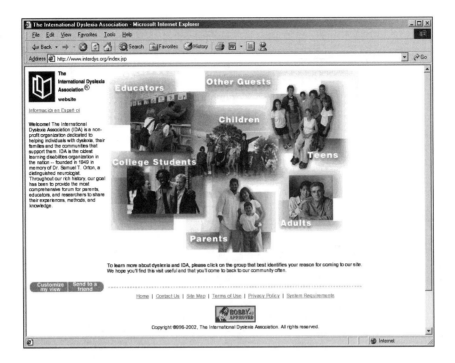

guage that may manifest itself in an imperfect ability to listen, think, speak, read, write, spell, or to do mathematical calculations. It includes conditions such as perceptual disabilities, brain injury, minimal brain dysfunction, dyslexia, and developmental aphasia. The term does not include learning problems that are primarily the result of visual, hearing, or motor disabilities, of mental retardation, of emotional disturbance, or of environmental, cultural, or economic disadvantage.

International Dyslexia Society

http://www.interdys.org

The International Dyslexia Association (IDA) (formerly The Orton Dyslexia Society) is an international, 501(c)(3) nonprofit, scientific and educational organization dedicated to the study and treatment of dyslexia.

Internet Special Education Resources

http://www.iser.com

Nationwide directory of professionals who serve learning disabilities and special education communities in assessment, placements, therapy, advocacy.

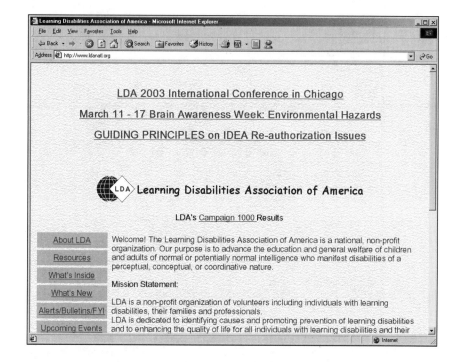

The Learning Disabilities Association of America

http://www.ldanatl.org

LDA is a national, nonprofit organization whose purpose is to advance the education and general welfare of children and adults of normal or potentially normal intelligence who manifest disabilities of a perceptual, conceptual, or coordinative nature.

LD Online

http://www.ldonline.org

This interactive guide to learning disabilities for parents, students, and teachers offers newsletters, teaching tips, and more.

National Center for Learning Disabilities, Inc.

http://www.ncld.org

News, links, resources for families and professionals.

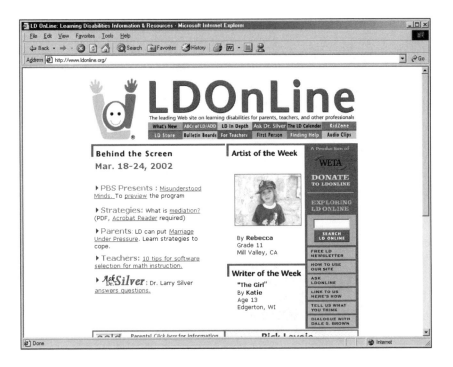

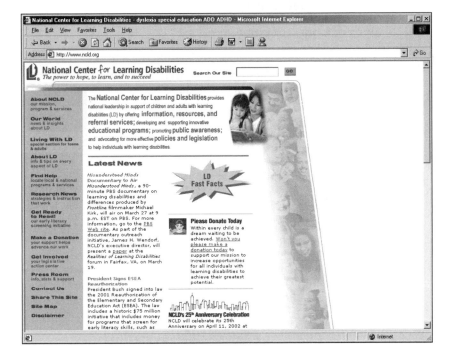

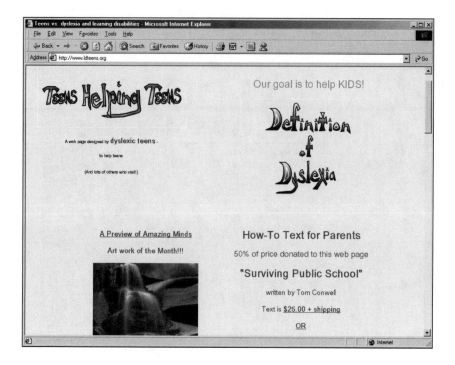

Teens Helping Teens

http://www.ldteens.org

This site was developed by teens with dyslexia to help others with dyslexia gain knowledge, a positive self-image, and a forum for expression. It also has sections for parents and teachers.

The Schwab Foundation for Learning

http://www.schwablearning.org

This foundation offers a wide range of services and information for parents and educators to support and promote the lives of children with learning differences.

SPEECH OR LANGUAGE IMPAIRMENT

Speech or language impairment means a communication disorder, such as stuttering, impaired articulation, a language impairment, or a voice impairment, that adversely affects a child's educational performance.

National Center for Stuttering

http://www.stuttering.com

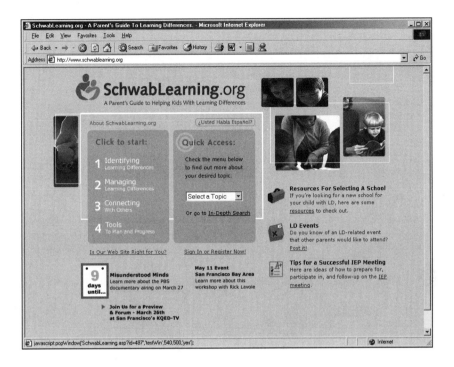

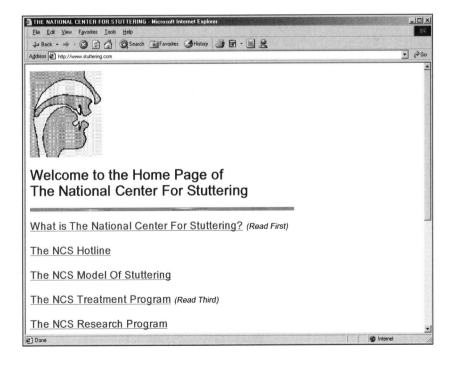

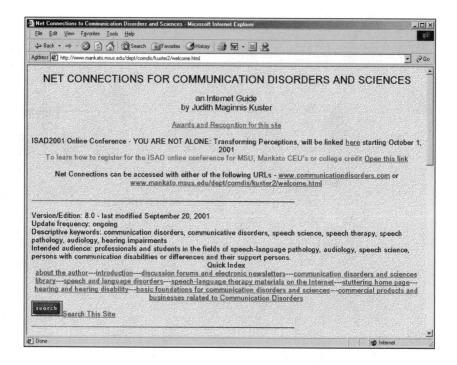

The National Center For Stuttering provides factual information about stuttering, a National Stutterer's Hotline, treatment for small groups of selected individuals who stutter, continuing education for speech pathologists, and research into the causes and treatment of stuttering.

Net Connections for Communication Disorders and Sciences

```
http://www.mankato.msus.edu/dept/comdis/kuster2/
welcome.html
```

Resources for professionals and students in communication disorders and sciences as well as for persons with communication disabilities and those who are part of their lives.

TRAUMATIC BRAIN INJURY

Traumatic brain injury means an acquired injury to the brain caused by an external physical force, resulting in total or partial functional disability or psychosocial impairment, or both. The term applies to open or closed head injuries resulting in impairments in one or more areas, such as cognition; language; memory; attention; reasoning; abstract thinking; judgment; problem-solving; sensory, perceptual, and motor abilities; psychosocial behav-

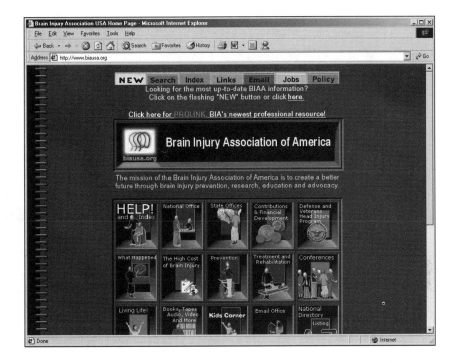

ior; physical functions; information processing; and speech. The term does not apply to brain injuries that are congenital or degenerative, or to brain injuries induced by birth trauma.

The Brain Injury Association, Inc.

`http://www.biausa.org`

Prevention, treatment and rehabilitation, kid's corner, living life after a brain injury, many resources including books, tapes, videos, and links to other Web sites.

Curry School of Education Resources on Traumatic Brain Injury

`http://curry.edschool.virginia.edu/go/cise/ose/categories/tbi.html`

The Whole Brain Atlas

`http://www.med.harvard.edu/AANLIB/home.html`

Harvard Medical Center presents a collection of images of human brains; contains a guided tour of neuroimaging and sections explaining the normal brain, as well as various medical conditions from Alzheimer's to stroke.

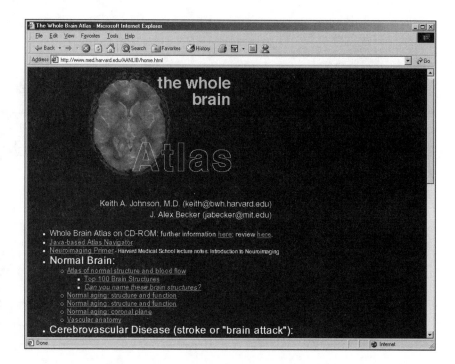

VISUAL IMPAIRMENT INCLUDING BLINDNESS

Visual impairment including blindness means an impairment in vision that, even with correction, adversely affects a child's educational performance. The term includes both partial sight and blindness.

American Council of the Blind (ACB)

http://www.acb.org

ACB strives to improve the well-being of people who are blind or visually impaired. This site offers *The Braille Forum* (a free monthly magazine), forums, helpful resources, radio, programs, and more.

Assistive Technology for People Who Are Blind or Visually Impaired

http://www.disabilityresources.org/AT-BLIND.html

A Disability Resources Monthly guide to the best online resources about assistive technology for people who are blind or have visual impairments.

Research Navigator Guide: Special Education

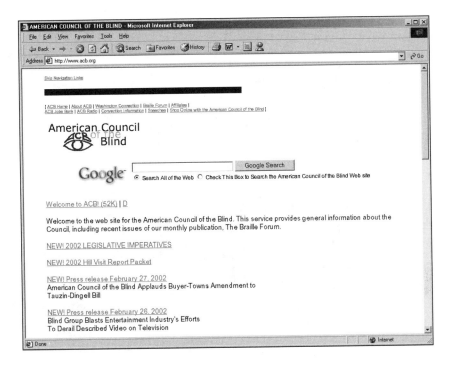

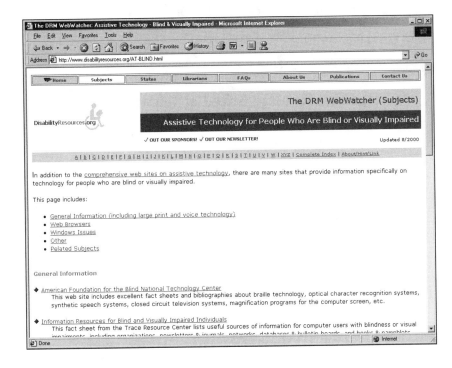

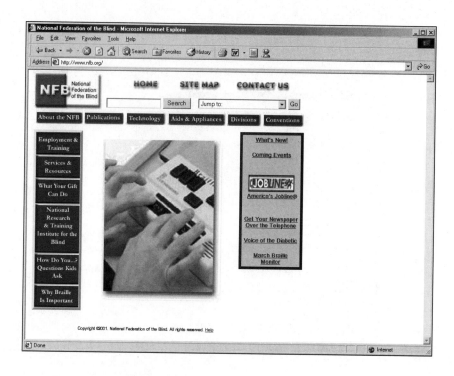

National Federation for the Blind

`http://www.nfb.org`

Links to news, events, research, jobline, resources.

Students Who Are Gifted or Talented

Giftedness is not a category of exceptionality under federal special education law. Nevertheless, several states provide specially designed instruction to students who are gifted and talented. There are many Web resources pertaining to giftedness that may be helpful to parents and teachers.

Belin & Blank International Center for Gifted Education and Talent Development

`http://www.uiowa.edu/~belinctr`

The State of Iowa Board of Regents established the center at the University of Iowa in June 1988. A leader in the field of gifted education, the center is known for its research, training, and service.

Gifted Resource Council

`http://www.cybam.com/grc`

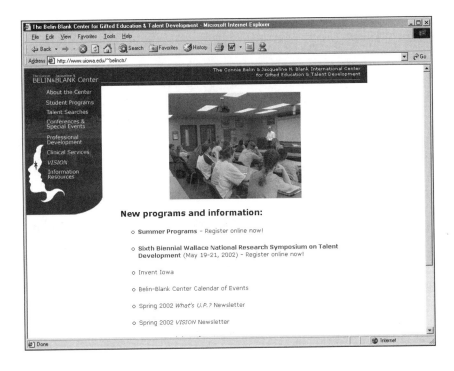

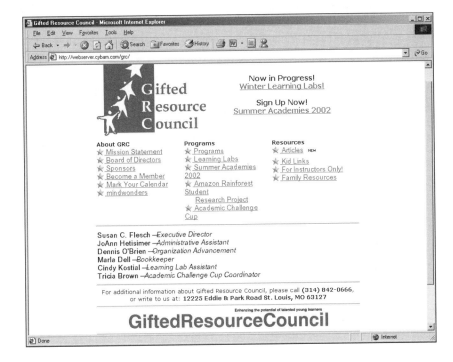

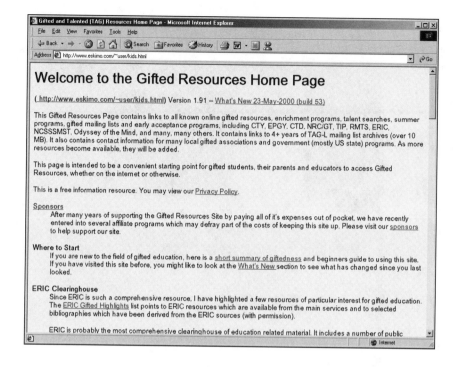

The Gifted Resource Council is a not-for-profit education agency based in St. Louis and dedicated to helping bright and talented children achieve their potential. The Web site contains resources for students, families, and teachers.

The Gifted and Talented Resources Home Page

http://www.eskimo.com/~user/kids.html

This Gifted Resources Page contains links to online gifted resources, enrichment programs, talent searches, summer programs, gifted mailing lists, and early acceptance programs. It also contains contact information for many local gifted associations and government programs.

National Association for Gifted Children

http://www.nagc.org

General information about NAGC, policy papers, publications and materials, parenting information, and state/federal information.

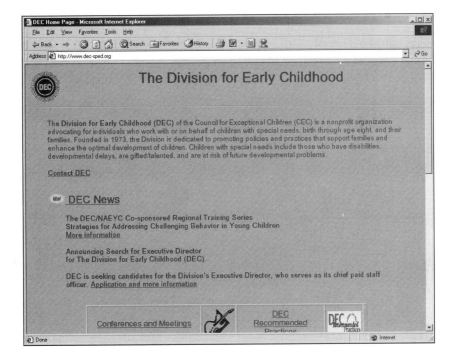

Early Childhood

States may provide special education services to children who are three through nine years old, not only under the categories of disability already described, but also if they are experiencing developmental delays in physical, cognitive, communication, social or emotional, or adaptive development.

Division for Early Childhood, Council for Exceptional Children

`http://www.dec-sped.org`

Information for educators and families of young children with special needs; includes publications, conferences, legal information, and links to other sites.

National Early Childhood Technical Assistance System

`http://www.nectas.unc.edu`

NECTAS is a national technical assistance consortium working to support states, jurisdictions, and others to improve services and results for young children with disabilities and their families.

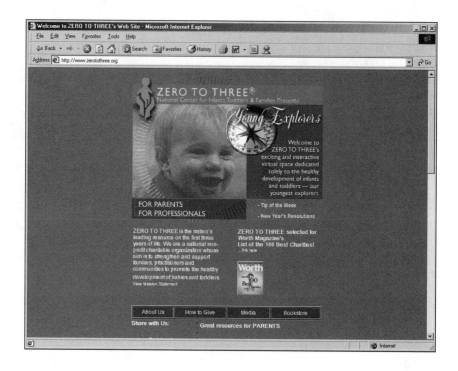

Toy Catalog Listing for Children with Special Needs

http://www.nas.com/downsyn/toy.html

Toys listed by title, links to producers; mailing list.

Zero to Three: National Center for Infants, Toddlers, and Families

http://www.zerotothree.org

Zero to three is an interactive Web site for parents and professionals. It includes a special section on how the brain develops, within the context of relationships, from conception through three years of age.

Transition to Adulthood

Under the IDEA, transition services must be provided for students with disabilities to promote movement from school to post-school activities, including postsecondary education, vocational training, integrated employment (including supported employment), continuing and adult education, adult services, independent living, or community participation.

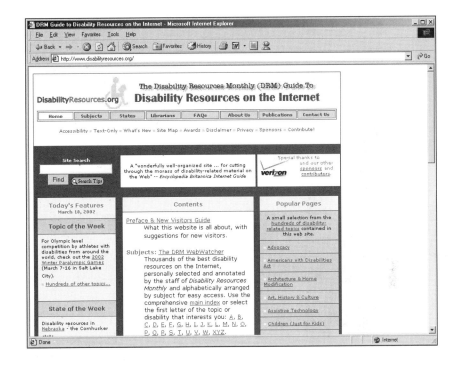

The DRM Guide to Disability Resources on the Internet

`http://www.disabilityresources.org`

Disability Resources Monthly provides comprehensive and easy-to-find information on resources related to independent living.

ETA disAbility Online

`http://wdsc.doleta.gov/disability`

The U.S. Department of Labor, Employment, and Training Administrations' disAbility Web site provides information on accessibility and removing barriers to employment encountered by adults with disabilities.

HEATH Resource Center

`http://www.heath.gwu.edu`

The HEATH Resource Center of the American Council on Education is the national clearinghouse on postsecondary education for individuals with disabilities. Support from the U.S. Department of Education enables HEATH to serve as an information exchange about educational support services, policies, procedures, adaptations, and opportunities at American

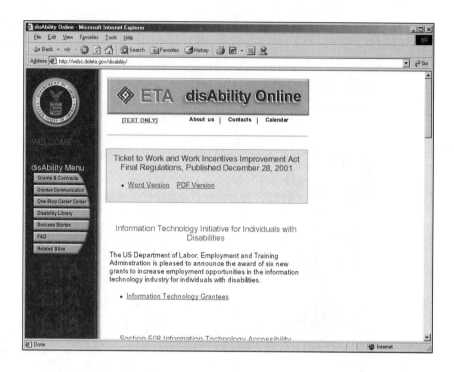

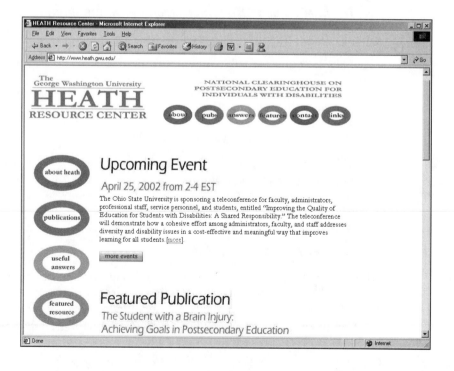

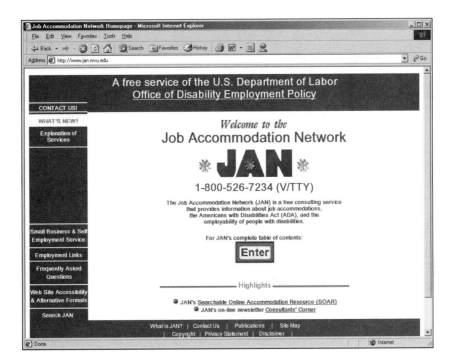

campuses, vocational-technical schools, and other postsecondary training entities.

Job Accommodation Network

http://www.jan.wvu.edu

Service of the President's Committee on Employment of People with Disabilities; publications, facts about job accommodations.

National Center on Secondary Education and Transition

http://ici.umn.edu/ncset

Publications, resources, searchable databases, model programs.

The School to Work Outreach Project (STWOP)

http://www.ici.coled.umn.edu/schooltowork

STWOP, funded by the U.S. Department of Education, presents profiles of exemplary school-to-work models/practices/strategies.

Research Navigator Guide: Special Education

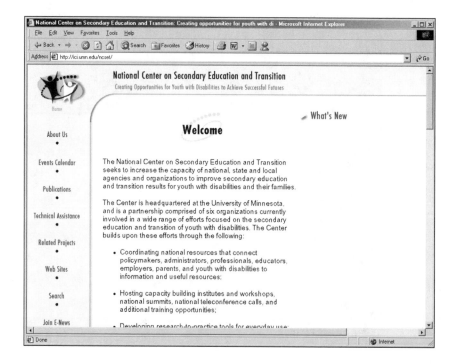

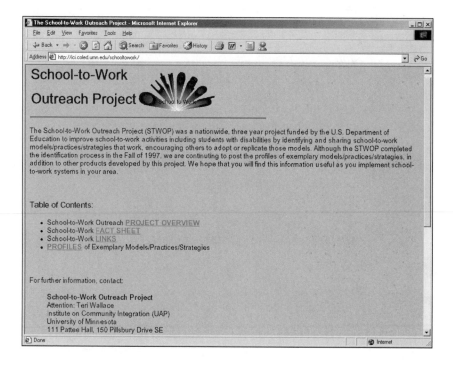

Tools for Teachers

The Internet contains many tools for both general education and special education teachers. In it you can find resources for your classroom, lesson plans and ideas from seasoned teachers, as well as ideas for collaborating with other teachers, parents, and auxiliary support personnel (paraprofessionals, school psychologists, and medical professionals). You can also find tips for writing Individualized Education Programs (IEPs), developing behavior change plans and performing functional behavior analysis as required under federal law.

FUNCTIONAL BEHAVIORAL ANALYSIS AND BEHAVIORAL CHANGE PLANS

Under the discipline provisions of the 1997 Amendments to the IDEA, schools must address the problem behaviors of students with disabilities. The following Web sites provide assistance to educators in evaluating problem behavior and designing behavioral interventions.

The Child Psychologist

`http://www.childpsychology.com/fba_bip`

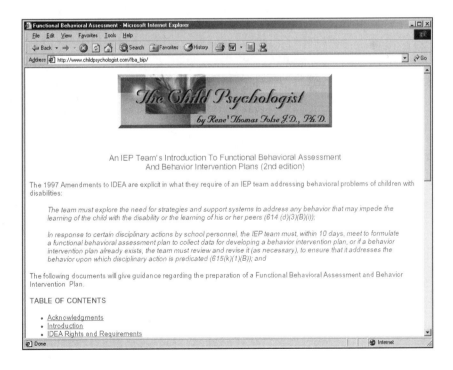

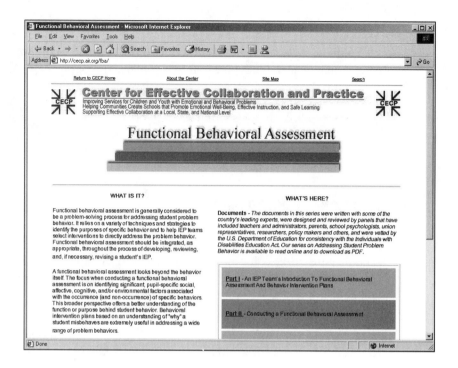

This Web site provides comprehensive information for IEP teams on functional behavioral assessment and behavior intervention plans.

Functional Behavior Assessment Mini Web

http://www.air-dc.org/cecp/fba

An IEP team's introduction to functional behavior assessment and behavior change plans; how to conduct a functional behavior assessment.

Multimodal Functional Behavioral Assessment Behavior Intervention Plans

http://mfba.net

This site provides an introduction to functional behavioral assessment online.

Positive Behavioral Interventions and Support

http://www.pbis.org

A technical assistance center established by the U.S. Office of Special Education Programs to give assistance to schools and teachers in developing school-wide positive behavioral interventions and support.

Research Navigator Guide: Special Education

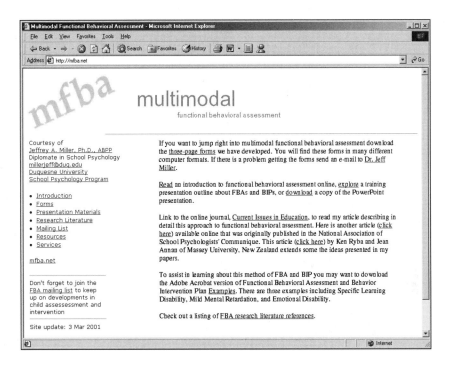

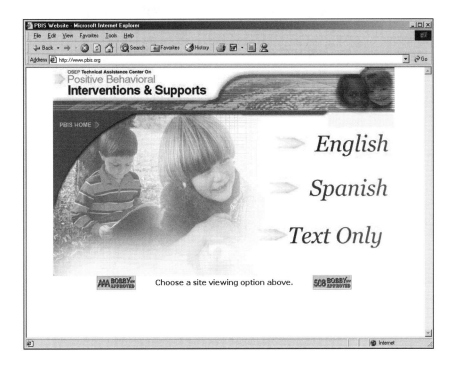

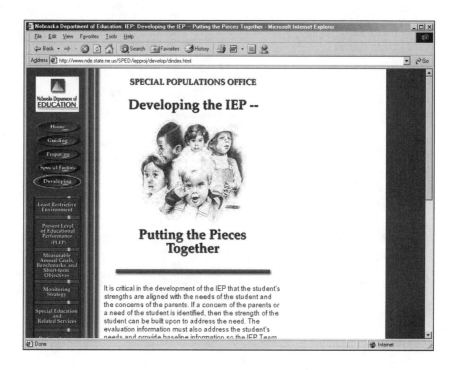

PLANNING AND IMPLEMENTING INDIVIDUALIZED EDUCATION PROGRAMS

Developing the IEP: Putting the Pieces Together

http://nde4.nde.state.ne.us/SPED/iepproj/
develop/dindex.html

Wondering about the difference between a benchmark and an objective? How to write present level statements or annual goals? In this site the Nebraska Department of Education presents a technical assistance guide for teachers, which explains the major aspects of IEP development.

Guide to the Individualized Education Program

http://www.ed.gov/offices/OSERS/OSEP/Products/
IEP_Guide

The Office of Special Education Programs from the U.S. Department of Education put together this excellent resource for parents and educators about the IEP and the basic special education process under federal law. This site would be an excellent starting place for general education teachers who want to understand how special education works.

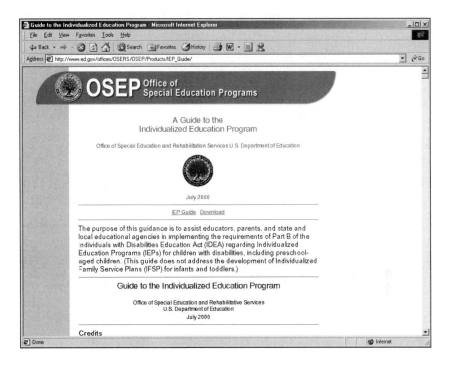

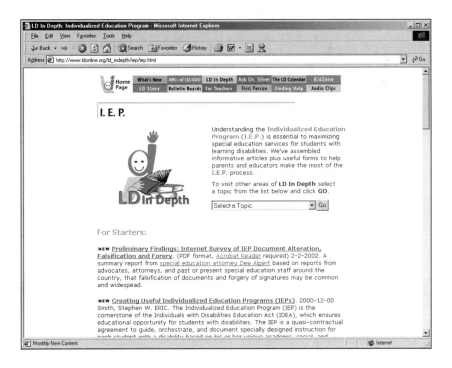

LD in Depth: Individualized Education Program

`http://www.ldonline.org/ld_indepth/iep/iep.html`

This site contains many links to help parents and teachers develop an IEP.

INCLUSION RESOURCES

Under the provision of placement in the "least restrictive environment," federal laws mandate that students with disabilities be integrated with nondisabled students to the maximum extent appropriate. The word "inclusion," which is not a legal term, is a synonym for integration of children with disabilities. The following resources will help general and special education teachers support children with disabilities in integrated settings.

Circle of Inclusion

`http://circleofinclusion.org`

A Web site for early childhood service providers and families of young children with disabilities provides information about effective practices of inclusive educational programs for your children.

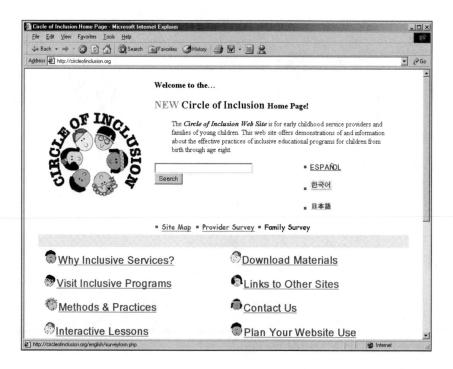

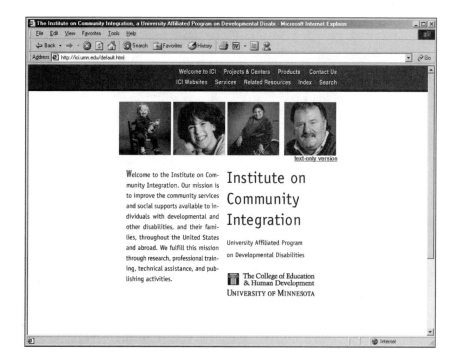

Institute on Community Integration

http://www.ici.coled.umn.edu/ici

Research, training, publications, resources.

The Inclusion Network

http://inclusion.org

The Inclusion Network is a Cincinnati-based nonprofit group with the goal of increasing integration of persons with disabilities at school, at work, and in their communities. Provides background information on inclusion including the legislative mandates for inclusion. An inspirational site!

Inclusion Education Resources

http://www.quasar.ualberta.ca/ddc/inclusion/intro.htm

A handbook for elementary, middle school, and secondary teachers provides support, organization tips, curriculum suggestions and modifications, and ideas for setting up a classroom for success.

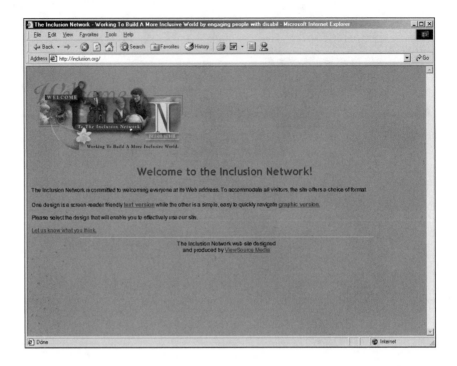

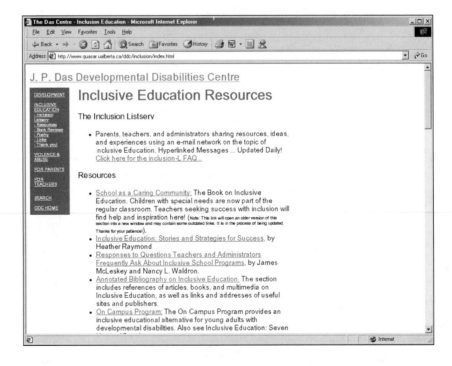

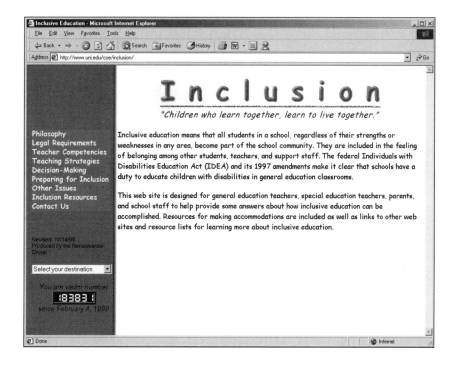

The What's and How To's of Inclusive Education

http://www.uni.edu/coe/inclusion

Provides current inclusion issues for general education and special education teachers. This site also provides resources for making accommodations. "Children who learn together, learn to live together."

LESSON PLANS AND MORE

21st Century Schoolhouse

http://www.coedu.usf.edu/~morris

Activities which accommodate different intelligences in the classroom; categories of information include educational links, worksheets, newspapers in education, lesson plans, and spelling ticklers.

AskERIC

http://ericir.syr.edu

Need to know the latest information on special education, curriculum development or other education topics? Just AskERIC! When you submit your education question to Q&A, you'll receive a personal email within two business days! The virtual library contains selected educational resources, including lesson plans, InfoGuides, searchable archives of education-related listservs, links to television series companion guides, and much more! The ERIC database, the world's largest source of education information, contains more than one million abstracts of documents and journal articles on education research and practice.

Blue Web'n

http://www.kn.pacbell.com/wired/bluewebn

A library of Blue Ribbon learning sites on the Web. Reviews and provides links to hundreds and hundreds of lesson plans, activities, projects, references, and other resources on the Internet.

Education World

http://www.education-world.com

Searchable database of more than 50,000 sites related to curriculum ideas. Many resources are geared specifically toward children with exceptionalities.

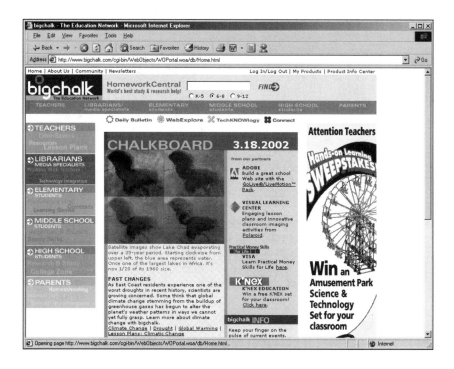

Bigchalk: The Education Network

`http://www.bigchalk.com`

A resource for anyone interested in learning about disabilities. The site offers teachers and parents guidelines on identifying children with learning and physical disabilities. It also provides lesson plans with modifications to assist the general education teacher.

Kathy Schrock's Guide for Educators

`http://school.discovery.com/schrockguide`

A categorized list of sites on the Internet useful for enhancing curriculum and teacher professional growth.

KidLink: Empowering Kids and Youth to Build Global Networks of Friends

`http://www.kidlink.org/english/general/index.html`

Students in 141 countries talk with each other about issues and present their ideas via electronic mail (email), a chat forum with live message exchange, and other types of communication, including "snail mail."

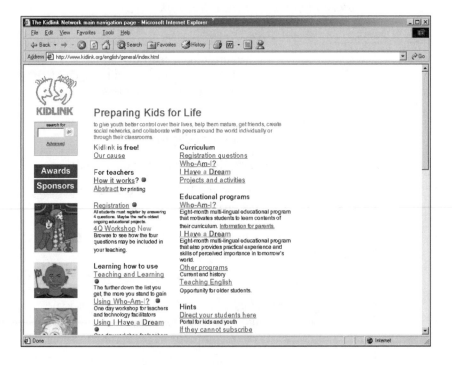

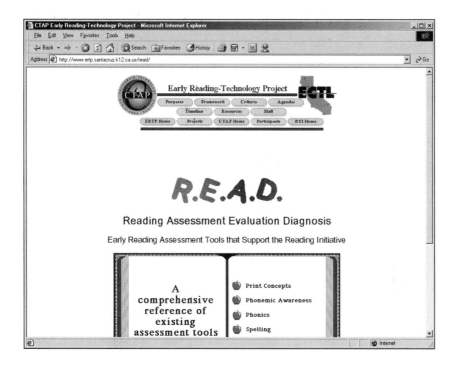

Reading Assessment Evaluation Diagnosis (R.E.A.D.)

http://www.ertp.santacruz.k12.ca.us/read/index.htm

Reading assessment tools for teachers of students who are in the early stages of reading, including sample assessments of print concepts, phonemic awareness, phonics, spelling, vocabulary development, and comprehension.

ReadWriteSite

http://www.readwrite.f2s.com

This Web site contains many resources for teachers and parents working with children who are learning to read. It includes a reading level estimator, lists of teacher-recommended books by reading or interest level, sight word lists, and literacy links.

The Special Needs Education (SNE) Project

http://www.schoolnet.ca/sne

Provides resources such as lesson plans, diagnostic tools, and other teaching and learning information.

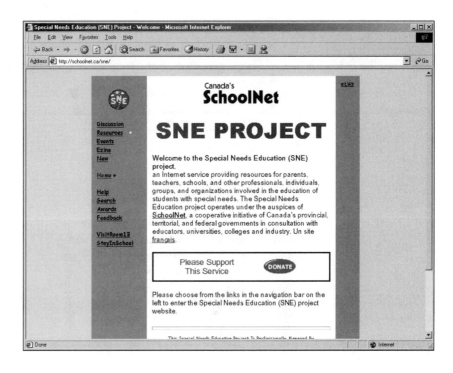

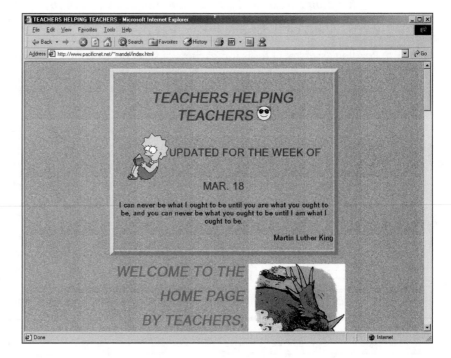

Teachers Helping Teachers

`http://www.pacificnet.net/~mandel/index.html`

Teachers around the country contribute the activities, for students from kindergarten through high school, to this site. The special education section contains a number of activities that are geared toward teaching basic skills to students with disabilities.

TeacherVision: The Learning Network Teacher Channel

`http://teachervision.com`

TeacherVision provides supplemental materials related to pre-K–12 curriculum and enrichment, including lesson plans, activities, and tools. The Special Needs section, developed in partnership with the Council for Exceptional Children (CEC), offers materials on ADD/ADHD, IEPs, inclusion, classroom management, and an archive of articles and resources on various topics, including a section on classroom adaptations and accommodations.

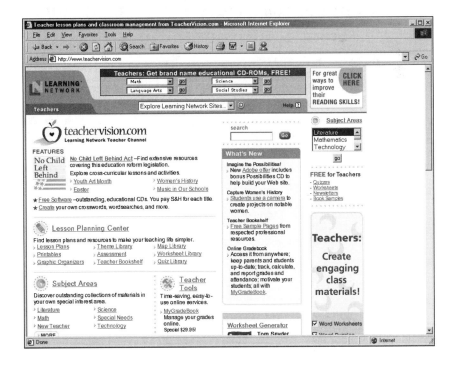

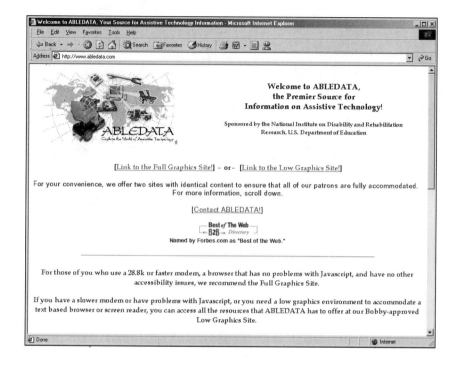

ASSISTIVE TECHNOLOGY FOR STUDENTS WITH DISABILITIES

Abledata

`http://www.abledata.com`

ABLEDATA is a service of The National Institute on Disability and Rehabilitation Research (U.S. Department of Education). Looking for an assistive technology product? Whether it's a simple, low-tech device or a
sophisticated computerized product, you'll probably find it in ABLEDATA's
searchable database of approximately 23,000 assistive devices. You'll also
find some invaluable fact sheets, consumer guides, and related material on
this Web site.

Alliance for Technology Access

`http://www.ataccess.org`

Grassroots national organization to provide information/resources to parents and professionals on disabilities and technology.

Apple Disability Resources

`http://www.apple.com/disability`

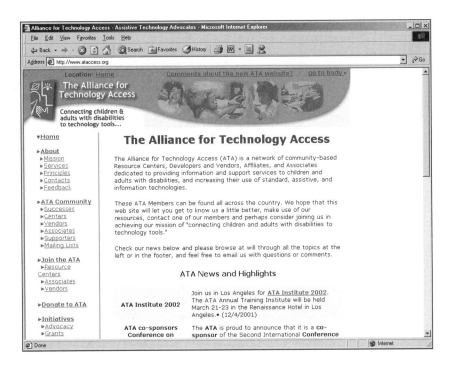

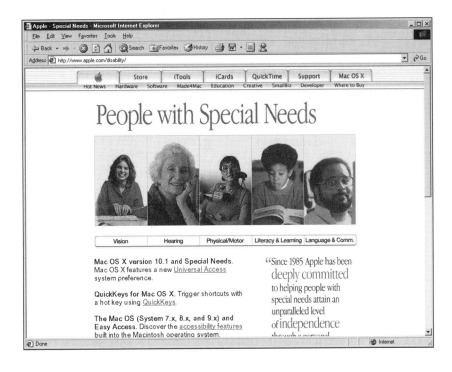

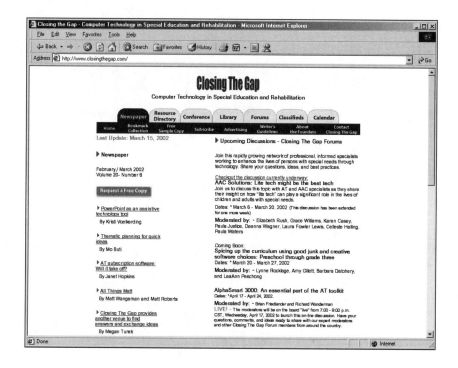

This site features a software library of freeware and shareware, a database of hundreds of disability products for the Macintosh, and information on Macintosh technologies.

Closing the Gap

http://www.closingthegap.com

Resource Guide to software and hardware, newspaper, articles, conferences related to computer technology in special education and rehabilitation.

Dreamms for Kids

http://www.dreamms.org

This assistive technology information clearinghouse is committed to increasing the use of computers and assistive technologies for students with special needs. The site has articles and products for special needs.

Microsoft's Accessibility Web Site

http://www.microsoft.com/enable

Information on technology and accessibility aids such as screen enlargers, screen reviews, on-screen keyboards, and voice input devices.

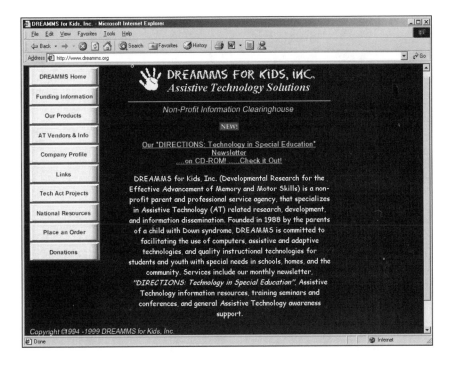

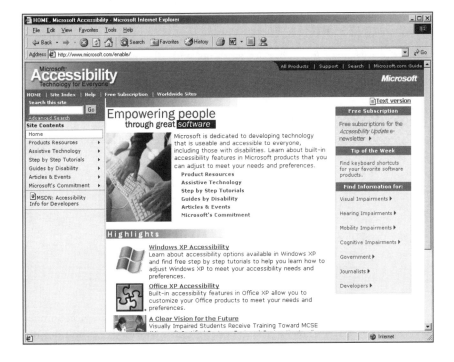

National Center to Improve Practice

http://www2.edc.org/NCIP

Provides a broad range of resources on assistive and instructional technologies for teachers of students with disabilities.

Recording for the Blind and Dyslexic

http://www.rfbd.org

RFBD is a national nonprofit organization that serves people who cannot read standard print because of a visual, perceptual, or other physical disability. The site includes an online catalogue of books and how to get involved as a reader. There are also many links to additional information about visual impairments and other disabilities.

PROFESSIONAL ORGANIZATIONS

American Academy on Pediatrics

http://www.aap.org

The mission of the American Academy of Pediatrics is to attain optimal physical, mental, and social health and well-being for all infants, children,

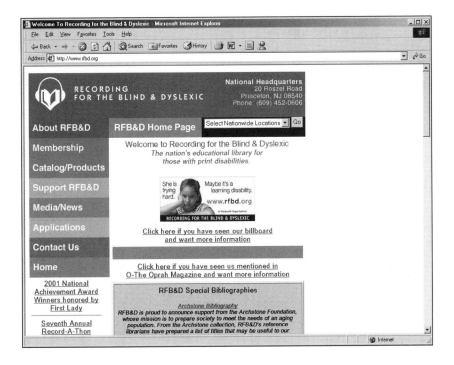

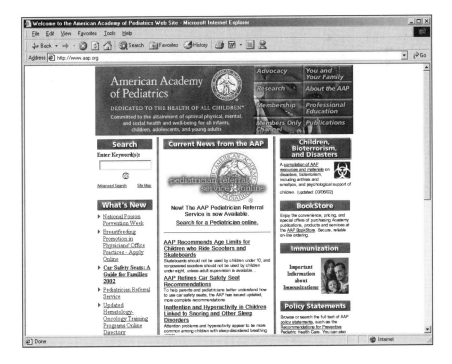

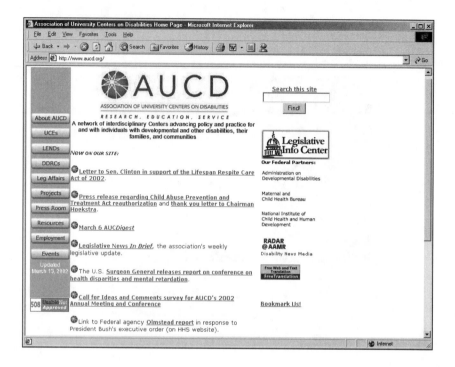

adolescents and young adults. Among other policies, read the guidelines of the AAP on the diagnosis of Attention Deficit Disorder (**http://www. aap.org/policy/AC0002.html**).

Association of University Centers on Disabilities

http://www.aauap.org

Authorized by the Developmental Disabilities Assistance and Bill of Rights Act (P.L. 104-183), UCDs are found in every state and territory of the U.S. Each is affiliated with a major research university. Visit this Web site to see what they have to offer in the way of academic training, technical assistance, services to the community, and research projects.

American Association on Mental Retardation

http://www.aamr.org

AAMR is a professional advocacy organization that was founded in 1876 to deal with life issues of persons with mental retardation. Its mission is to promote global development and dissemination of progressive policies, sound research, effective practices, and universal human rights for people

with intellectual disabilities. Non-members can read old copies of the newsletter, visit the bookstore, or participate in online discussions.

American Psychological Association

`http://www.apa.org`

Based in Washington, DC, the American Psychological Association (APA) is the largest scientific and professional organization representing psychology in the United States. APA is also the largest association of psychologists worldwide. The Web site contains many resources for the public and for students. Software on APA style of writing is available online for new writers in the behavioral sciences.

American Speech-Language-Hearing Association

`http://www.asha.org`

ASHA is the professional, scientific, and credentialing association for more than 97,000 audiologists, speech-language pathologists, and speech, language, and hearing scientists. This site is a resource for ASHA members, persons interested in information about communication disorders, and for those wanting career and membership information.

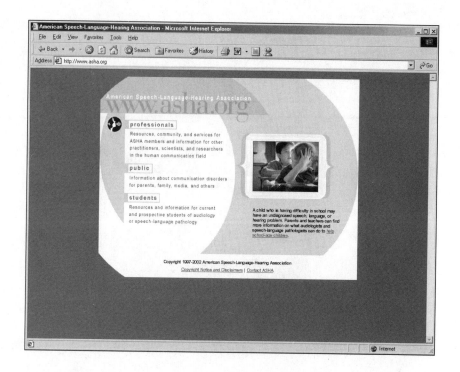

Association on Higher Education and Disability (AHEAD)

`http://www.ahead.org`

AHEAD is an organization of professionals committed to full participation in higher education for persons with disabilities. The Web site provides access to a collection of links useful to postsecondary students with disabilities and educators in higher education.

The Council for Exceptional Children

`http://www.cec.sped.org`

The Council for Exceptional Children (CEC) is the largest international professional organization dedicated to improving educational outcomes for individuals with exceptionalities, students with disabilities, and/or the gifted. CEC advocates for appropriate governmental policies, sets professional standards, provides continual professional development, advocates for newly and historically underserved individuals with exceptionalities, and helps professionals obtain conditions and resources necessary for effective professional practice.

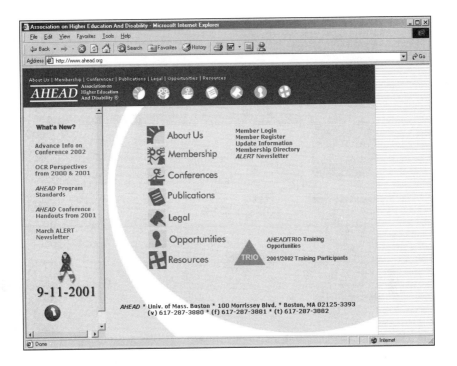

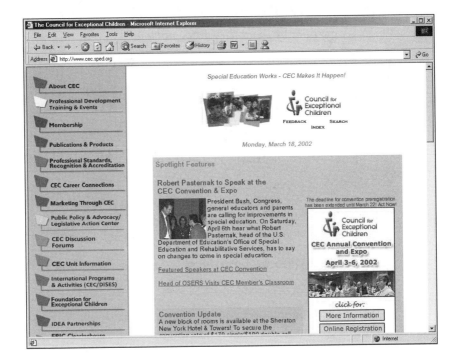

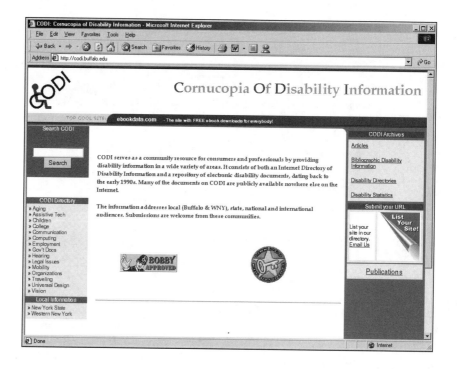

Resources for Parents and Families

Cornucopia of Disability Information

http://codi.buffalo.edu

CODI provides disability information in a wide variety of areas. "Traveling with a Disability" contains a particularly useful set of links for families.

Disability Resources Monthly (DRM)

http://www.disabilityresources.org

This Web site provides access to the DRM WebWatcher, an easy-to-use on-line subject guide to disability resources on the Internet, and the DRM Regional Resource Directory, a guide to state and local agencies and organizations.

Family & Advocates Partnership in Education (FAPE)

http://www.fape.org

FAPE aims to inform and educate families about the Individuals with Disabilities Education Act of 1997. This site has information on FAPE's goals, a calendar, laws and regulations, associated links, and more.

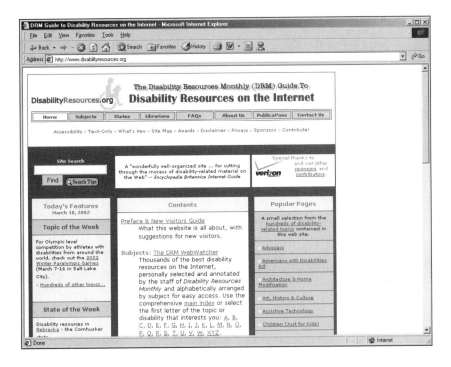

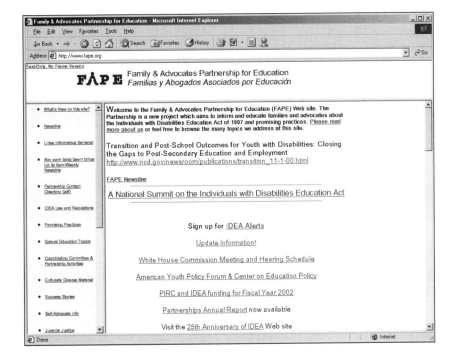

Familyeducation.com

`http://familyeducation.com`

As part of The Learning Network, Familyeducation.com addresses the needs and concerns of parents of exceptional children and the educators who serve them. TLN is an online community of parents, teachers, and school dedicated to children's learning. The network includes *familyeducation. com* for parents, *teachervision.com* for teachers, and *myschoolonline.com* for school-home communication.

Family Friendly Fun with Special Needs

`http://www.family-friendly-fun.com`

Created by the family of a child with special needs, this Web site is described as containing mind, body and spirit-enriching resources to enhance the quality and enjoyment of family life with special needs. It covers a wide range of topics from arts and crafts to vacations.

Family Village

`http://www.familyvillage.wisc.edu`

A global community of information, resources, and communication opportunities for persons with mental retardation and other disabilities; includes

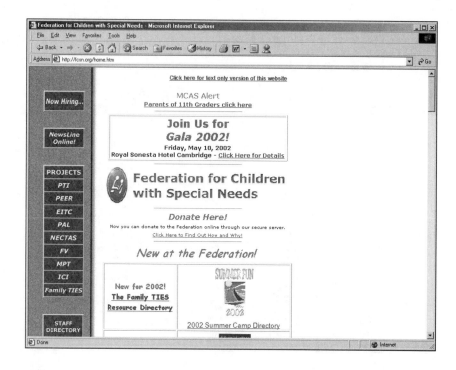

informational resources on specific disabilities, communication connections, adaptive products and technology, adaptive recreational activities, education, worship, health issues, disability-related media and literature, and much, much more.

Federation for Children with Special Needs

`http://www.fcsn.org/home.htm`

Massachusetts-based resource center for parents.

HalfthePlanet

`http://www.halftheplanet.com`

A Web site where the disability community can access reliable services and products, connect with peer support, and keep up with disability-related news and information.

National Fathers Network

`http://www.fathersnetwork.org`

NFN, a nonprofit organization providing support and resources to fathers and families with special needs children, provides articles, resources, links, and a photo album at their site.

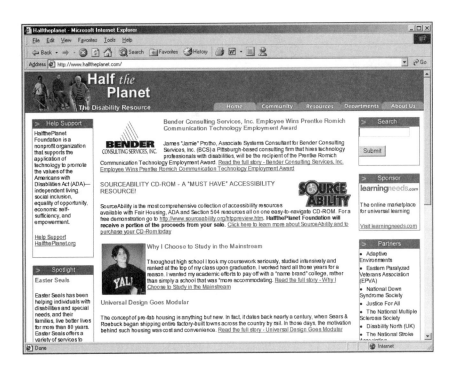

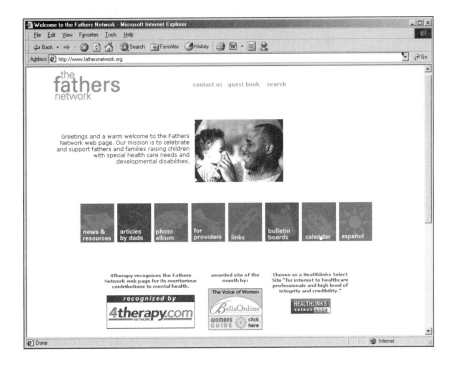

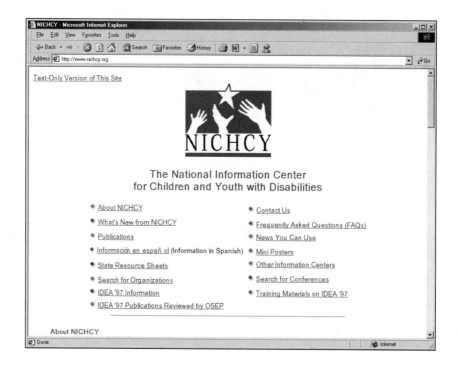

National Information Center for Children and Youth with Disabilities (NICHCY)

http://www.nichcy.org

The National Information Center for Children and Youth with Disabilities is the national information and referral center that provides information on disabilities and disability-related issues for families, educators, and other professionals.

National Parent Information Network

http://www.npin.org

NPIN is a project of the ERIC system which is administered by the National Library of Education in the U.S. Department of Education; parent news, searchable database; a virtual library with full-text articles, summaries of books, and descriptions of newsletters and magazines.

National Parent Network on Disabilities

http://www.npnd.org/main.htm

NPND is a nonprofit advocacy organization dedicated to empowering parents. Located in Washington, DC, NPND provides up-to-date information

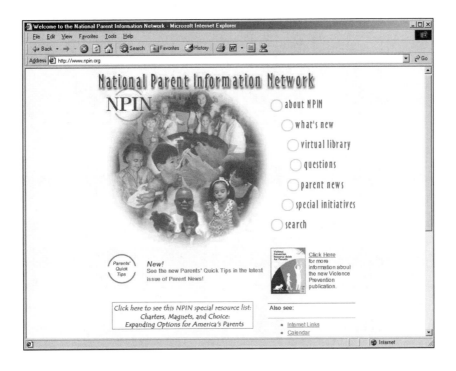

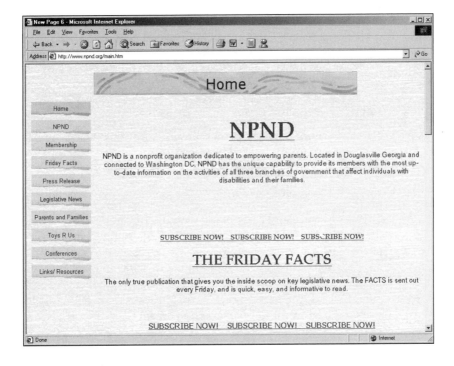

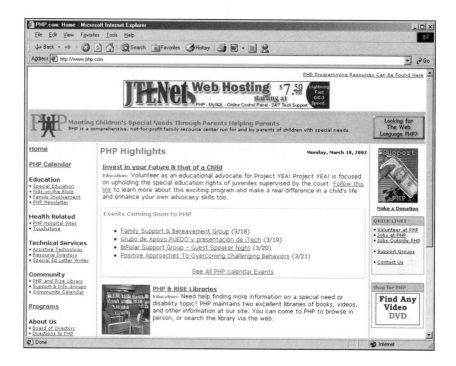

on the activities of all three branches of government that impact individuals with disabilities and their families. This Web site provides information on national parent training and information centers and community parent resource centers.

Parents Helping Parents

http://www.php.com

National parent resource center, programs, events, links.

Self-Advocates Becoming Empowered (SABE)

http://www.sabeusa.org/

SABE aims to ensure that people with disabilities are treated as equals and that they are given the same decisions, choices, rights, responsibilities, and chances to speak up to empower themselves. The organization's goals are to make self-advocacy available in every state, to work with the criminal justice system and people with disabilities about their rights within the criminal justice system, and to close institutions for people with developmental disabilities and build community supports.

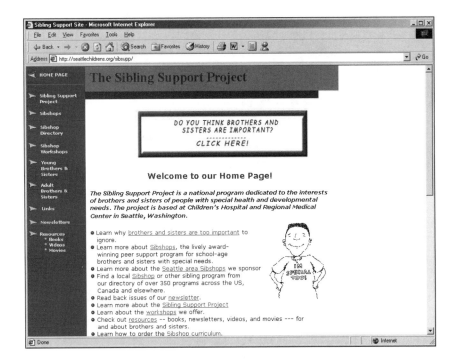

The Sibling Support Project

`http://www.seattlechildrens.org/sibsupp`

The Sibling Support Project is a national program dedicated to the interests of brothers and sisters of people with special health and developmental needs. The project is based at Children's Hospital and Regional Medical Center in Seattle, Washington.

Other Online Resources

Companion Web Sites

`http://www.abinteractive.com/gallery`

Our Companion Web sites use the Internet to provide you with various opportunities for further study and exploration. The CW offers study content and activities related to the text, as well as an interactive, online study guide. Quizzes containing multiple choice, true/false, and essay questions

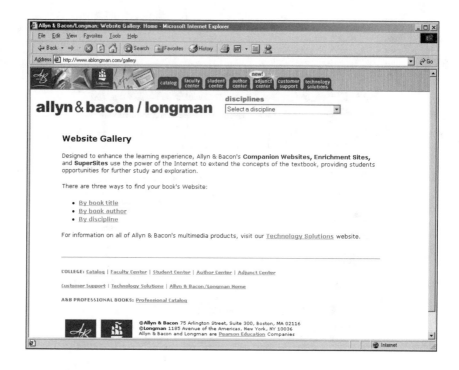

can be graded instantly, and forwarded to your instructor for recording—all online. For a complete list of titles with a CW, visit **www.abinteractive.com/gallery.**

Glossary

Your Own Private Glossary

The Glossary in this book contains reference terms you'll find useful as you get started on the Internet. After a while, however, you'll find yourself running across abbreviations, acronyms, and buzzwords whose definitions will make more sense to you once you're no longer a novice (or "newbie"). That's the time to build a glossary of your own. For now, the Webopedia gives you a place to start.

alias A simple email address that can be used in place of a more complex one.

AVI Audio Video Interleave. A video compression standard developed for use with Microsoft Windows. Video clips on the World Wide Web are usually available in both AVI and QuickTime formats.

bandwidth Internet parlance for capacity to carry or transfer information such as email and Web pages.

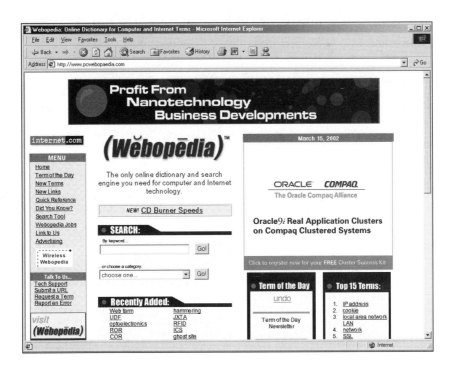

browser   The computer program that lets you view the contents of Web sites.

client   A program that runs on your personal computer and supplies you with Internet services, such as getting your mail.

cyberspace   The whole universe of information that is available from computer networks. The term was coined by science fiction writer William Gibson in his novel *Neuromancer,* published in 1984.

DNS   See *domain name server.*

domain   A group of computers administered as a single unit, typically belonging to a single organization such as a university or corporation.

domain name   A name that identifies one or more computers belonging to a single domain. For example, "apple.com".

domain name server   A computer that converts domain names into the numeric addresses used on the Internet.

download   Copying a file from another computer to your computer over the Internet.

email   Electronic mail.

emoticon   A guide to the writer's feelings, represented by typed characters, such as the Smiley :-). Helps readers understand the emotions underlying a written message.

FAQs   Frequently Asked Questions

flame   A rude or derogatory message directed as a personal attack against an individual or group.

flame war   An exchange of flames (see above).

ftp   File Transfer Protocol, a method of moving files from one computer to another over the Internet.

home page   A page on the World Wide Web that acts as a starting point for information about a person or organization.

hypertext   Text that contains embedded *links* to other pages of text. Hypertext enables the reader to navigate between pages of related information by following links in the text.

LAN   Local Area Network. A computer network that is located in a concentrated area, such as offices within a building.

link   A reference to a location on the Web that is embedded in the text of the Web page. Links are usually highlighted with a different color or underlined to make them easily visible.

listserv   Strictly speaking, a computer program that administers electronic mailing lists, but also used to denote such lists or

discussion groups, as in "the writer's listserv."

lurker   A passive reader of an Internet *newsgroup* or *listserv.* A lurker reads messages, but does not participate in the discussion by posting or responding to messages.

mailing list   A subject-specific automated email system. Users subscribe and receive email from other users about the subject of the list.

modem   A device for connecting two computers over a telephone line.

newbie   A new user of the Internet.

newsgroup   A discussion forum in which all participants can read all messages and public replies between the participants.

plug-in   A third-party software program that will lend a Web browser (Netscape, Internet Explorer, etc.) additional features.

quoted   Text in an email message or newsgroup posting that has been set off by the use of vertical bars or > characters in the left-hand margin.

search engine   A computer program that will locate Web sites or files based on specified criteria.

secure   A Web page whose contents are encrypted when sending or receiving information.

server   A computer program that moves information on request, such as a Web server that sends pages to your browser.

Smiley   See *emoticon.*

snail mail   Mail sent the old fashioned way: Write a letter, put it in an envelope, stick on a stamp, and drop it in the mailbox.

spam   Spam is to the Internet as unsolicited junk mail is to the postal system.

URL   Uniform Resource Locator: The notation for specifying addresses on the World Wide Web (e.g. http://www.abacon.com or ftp://ftp.abacon.com).

Usenet   The section of the Internet devoted to *newsgroups.*

Web browser   A program used to navigate and access information on the World Wide Web. Web browsers convert html coding into a display of pictures, sound, and words.

Web page   All the text, graphics, pictures, and so forth, denoted by a single URL beginning with the identifier "http://".

Web site   A collection of World Wide Web pages, usually consisting of a home page and several other linked pages.

Research Navigator Guide: Special Education